WELCOME TO SNOOPY'S WORLD

Based on the English Language Book "CHARLIE BROWN'S
'CYCLOPEDIA—VOLUMES 5, 10, 15" © 1990 United Feature Syndicate, Inc.

This 1994 edition is published by Derrydale Books,
distributed by Random House Value Publishing, Inc.,
40 Engelhard Avenue, Avenel, New Jersey 07001

Cover designed by Bill Akunevicz Jr.
Production supervised by Roméo Enriquez

Manufactured in the United States of America

Library of Congress Cataloging-in-Publication Data
Schulz, Charles M.
Earth, water, and air / Illustrated by Charles Schulz.
p.   cm.—(Snoopy's world)
First work originally published: Cars, trains, and other wheels. Funk and Wagnalls, 1992.
2nd work originally published: Boats and things that float. Funk and Wagnalls, 1992.
3rd work originally published: Planes and things that fly. Funk and Wagnalls, 1992.
ISBN 0-517-11897-1
1. Motor vehicles—Juvenile literature. 2. Earth sciences—Juvenile literature.
3. Astronomy—Juvenile literature. [1. Space flight. 2. Earth sciences. 3. Astronomy.]
I. Schulz, Charles M.   Cars, trains, and other wheels.   1994.
II. Schulz, Charles M.   Boats and things that float.
III. Schulz, Charles M.   Planes and things that fly.   1994.
IV. Title.   V. Series: Schulz, Charles M.   Snoopy's world.
TL147.S39   1994
629.04—dc20
94-15102
CIP   AC

10 9 8 7 6 5 4 3 2 1

EARTH, WATER AND AIR

Based on the Characters of Charles M. Schulz

Derrydale Books
New York • Avenel

INTRODUCTION

Welcome to Snoopy's World, where you will discover fascinating facts about cars and trains, boats and submarines, planes and even hot air balloons. Have you ever wondered when the bicycle was invented, or what a galleon is, or what the Red Baron really was? Charlie Brown, Snoopy, and the rest of the *Peanuts* gang are here to help you find the answers to these questions and many more about the way things work. Have fun!

CONTENTS

GOING UP?

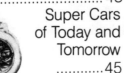

CONTENTS

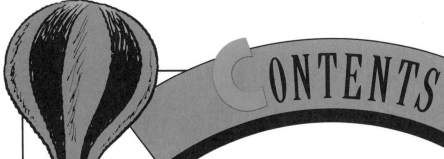

CONTENTS

Can you imagine a world without wheels? You couldn't take the bus to school. Your roller skates wouldn't roll. There wouldn't be any cars for a ride to the beach or the store. How did people get around before cars were invented?

A WORLD WITHOUT WHEELS

CHAPTER 1

WALKING

How did people travel long ago?

Before people knew of any other way to travel, they walked from place to place. Travel on foot was slow. When people wanted to go long distances, they often had to spend days, weeks, months—even years—getting there.

How were important messages delivered?

People often used special runners to deliver important messages. Once, in ancient Greece, a runner was sent from a city called Marathon all the way to Athens to announce a victory in war. The special 26-mile marathon race that people run today is named after this famous running event from ancient times.

A man recently walked around the entire globe. It took him more than three years to make the trip—including the time he traveled by boat when he came to large bodies of water!

Did rulers and wealthy people in ancient times travel on foot?

Probably not. In ancient Egypt, the Pharaohs (FAIR-oze), or kings, were carried on litters by slaves. The emperors of ancient Rome were also carried this way. A litter was a couch on two poles. Four slaves carried it by balancing the poles on their shoulders. While the slaves walked, the passenger could stretch out on the couch. There were so many litters in Rome, they caused traffic jams!

YOU SHOULD ALL CARRY ME ON A LITTER!

RIDING ON ANIMALS

In Egypt, camels are still used to carry people across the desert.

Why did people first ride on animals' backs?

Large animals such as horses, mules, and camels don't get tired as quickly as people. So when men, women, and children started to ride animals, they were able to travel long distances more quickly than before. They also saved energy by riding instead of walking.

What animals are used to carry people and things?

In the desert lands of Egypt and Syria, people use oxen, donkeys, and camels. Camels are especially good for desert travel because they can live for long periods without water. Reindeer are ideal for the people of icy Lapland, the northern part of Scandinavia. Reindeer move quickly in snow and can carry up to 300 pounds. Eskimos near the North Pole train dogs to pull sleds and carry light loads. In mountain areas, llamas are used because they are good climbers. They carry things for the Indians of Peru in the Andes Mountains.

SKIS, SKATES, AND SLEDS

When did people start using skis?

People have used skis for more than 5,000 years. Skiing began as a way of getting around in places where there was a lot of snow. The first skis were probably made from animal bones. Because they are long, flat, and smooth, skis glide easily over snow and ice.

What is cross-country skiing?

When you go cross-country skiing, you don't just go down hills. You may also ski uphill and across flat ground. Cross-country skiers use their leg muscles and swing their arms to push themselves along. They usually ski long distances, often on country trails. Their skis are narrower and lighter than downhill skis. Cross-country skis also have special ridges that grip the snow and help the skier move forward. In places where it snows often, people use cross-country skis to get around.

When did people first ice-skate?

No one knows exactly when people first started ice-skating, but they have been doing it for hundreds of years. Ice-skating was originally a way of traveling. The first ice skates were wooden runners strapped to shoes.

In the Netherlands today, there are many canals that freeze in the winter. People still skate many miles along the canals to get around.

Did people ever use sleds without snow?

Yes, and they still do today. The sled was one of the earliest vehicles. Vehicles are objects that carry people or things from one place to another. The earliest sleds were just flat pieces of wood dragged along the ground. Then people added wooden runners underneath. These were curved like the metal runners on a modern snow sled. Oxen and other large animals pulled the sleds.

Are sleds and sleighs the same?

These words sometimes mean the same thing. They are both vehicles on runners but we often think of a sled as being smaller than a sleigh. People usually use the word *sleigh* to mean a horse-drawn wagon in which people can ride.

What is a toboggan?

A toboggan is a vehicle without runners that glides on snow and ice. A toboggan is made of long strips of wood that curl up at the front. The underside of a toboggan is polished, so it glides easily and moves very fast.

American Indians made the first toboggans to carry things across snow. Today, people use toboggans mostly for an exciting ride down a hillside. There are even special toboggan trails where you can *soar* downhill over hard-packed snow!

CHAPTER 2

It's a perfect circle—and it's everywhere! We see wheels under cars, buses, trucks, and tractors. Machines we use every day need wheels to work. Clocks, doorknobs, and eggbeaters all use wheels! With the discovery of wheels, many new things were invented—especially vehicles. So let's take a trip with Charlie Brown and see how the wheel gave us exciting ways to get around.

THE AMAZING WHEEL

WHEELS, WHEELS, WHEELS

NO, I GUESS YOU DON'T NEED WHEELS WHEN YOU CAN FLY.

Who invented the wheel?

No one knows exactly who invented the wheel or when. We do know, however, that people were using it about 5,000 years ago in the areas now known as Iraq, Syria, and Turkey.

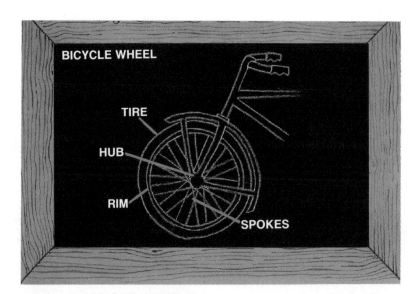

BICYCLE WHEEL

TIRE

HUB

RIM

SPOKES

What are the parts of a wheel called?

Here is a diagram of a wheel. The outer part of the wheel is called the *rim*. At the center of the wheel is the *hub*. The rim is connected to the hub by *spokes*. The spokes are what give a wheel its support.

What was the first wheel like?

The first wheels were probably round slices of a log. The idea for the wheel might have come from log "rollers." People used to place logs under a large object. Then they rolled the object across the logs. There was one problem with this method. As soon as the object passed over a log, the log had to be carried to the front of the object again.

Without the wheel we wouldn't have things such as cars, trains, airplanes, bicycles, watches, clocks, or washing machines!

CHARIOTS, CARRIAGES, COACHES, AND WAGONS

What was the first vehicle with wheels?

Probably the chariot. It was a two-wheeled cart, open at the back. At first, chariots were pulled by donkeys. Then people used horses to pull their chariots along. People who rode in chariots did not sit in them—they stood.

Ancient Greeks and Romans used chariots for fighting wars. Sometimes a soldier would stand in the chariot with the horse's reins tied to his waist. Then his hands were free to hold a spear and fight the enemy.

What were other early vehicles with wheels?

Around the same time that the chariot was invented, people started using four-wheeled wagons and two-wheeled carts. These new vehicles were used for carrying heavy loads.

What is a carriage?

A carriage is a vehicle built to carry seated people. Carriages were usually pulled by horses. Ancient Romans used carriages 2,000 years ago, but carriages were most popular in Europe and America in the 1700s and 1800s. During that time, carriages were light, fast, and graceful.

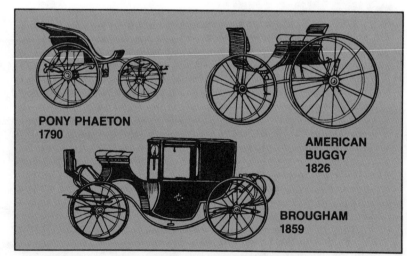

PONY PHAETON 1790

AMERICAN BUGGY 1826

BROUGHAM 1859

Are there different carriages?

Here are some pictures of a few kinds of carriages. They were all pulled by horses—from one to six, depending on the type of carriage.

How did it feel to ride in a cabriolet?

The cabriolet (cab-ree-uh-LAY) must have given a very gentle, bouncy ride. It was a lightweight carriage, but it had heavy-duty springs under the seat. When a trotting horse pulled the cabriolet over the unpaved roads of the 1800s, the carriage leaped in rhythm.

The French word *cabriolet* means "little leap." It comes from an older French word for baby goat. Riding in a cabriolet probably reminded someone of riding on the back of a playful baby goat.

VICTORIA CARRIAGE

What was a coach?

Do you remember Cinderella? She rode in a coach when she went to the ball. A coach was a large, four-wheeled carriage that was closed on the sides and on top.

After the 1500s, coaches were used in Europe for public transportation. Rich people owned their own coaches, but their rides were just as bumpy as everyone else's. Early roads were full of holes and bumps, and springs were not put under carriage seats until the late 1700s. Before then, even a king had a very rough ride when he traveled by coach!

Which carriage did rich people use?

The victoria and the landau were used by rich and royal Europeans. Some wealthy people in America also owned these carriages, which were made of fine woods and metals. From the outside, the landau looked like a jewel box on wheels. Inside, it often had velvet and satin seats and walls trimmed in gold. The landau's roof could be folded back or closed to keep out bad weather.

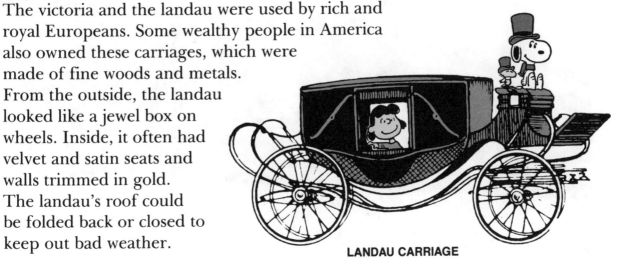

LANDAU CARRIAGE

17

What was a stagecoach?

A stagecoach was a coach that carried passengers. Four to eight people could sit inside the coach. Mail, packages, and luggage were placed on the roof.

Stagecoaches traveled on regular routes between two or more cities. The drivers changed horses at set stops, or "stages," along the routes. That's how stagecoaches got their name. These vehicles became popular in Europe in the late 1600s and in America in the late 1700s. One big problem faced by people who used stagecoaches was the threat of robbers. Poor roads and bad weather also made stagecoach travel uncomfortable and dangerous.

What did American pioneers use to travel west?

American pioneers moved west in covered wagons pulled by teams of horses. True to its name, a covered wagon was a rectangular wooden cart covered by a high canvas top that was stretched over curved wooden ribs. Pioneer families packed their household belongings inside these sturdy wagons. Usually groups of families traveled together. One behind the other, their wagons followed a trail. The long line of wagons was called a wagon train.

Covered wagons traveled in a group called a wagon train.

What is a prairie schooner?

A schooner (SKOO-nur) is a kind of sailing ship, but "prairie schooner" was a nickname for a covered wagon. People called it that because it "sailed" across the prairies or plains just as a schooner sails across the water.

BICYCLES

When were bicycles first invented?

In the late 1400s, the Italian artist and inventor Leonardo da Vinci made the first machine propelled by cranks and pedals, but it didn't look much like the bike you ride today. A French count, Comte Mede de Sivrac (med duh see-VRAHCK), built a wooden model in 1790. It had no pedals and no steering bar. A rider had to move and steer by putting his feet on the ground and pushing. De Sivrac's model was more like a "walking machine" than a bicycle.

In about 1816, a German, Baron Karl von Drais (fon DRICE), built a model with a steering bar. In 1839, foot pedals were finally added by a Scottish blacksmith named Kirkpatrick Macmillan. This bicycle was much more like the ones we see today.

An early bicycle, called a penny-farthing, had a front wheel about nine times larger than the back wheel!

SO, WHO INVENTED BICYCLES, ANYWAY?

19

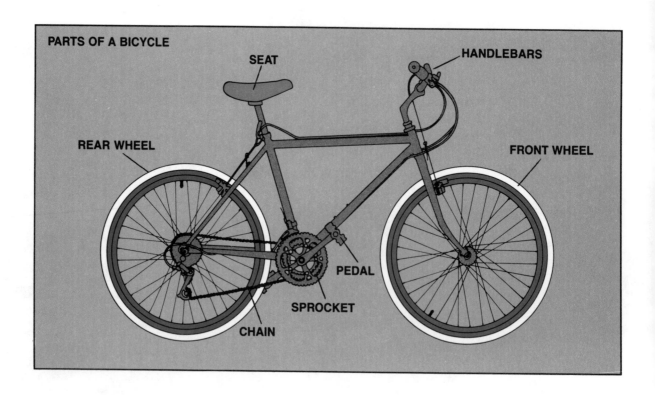

PARTS OF A BICYCLE

SEAT

HANDLEBARS

REAR WHEEL

FRONT WHEEL

PEDAL

SPROCKET

CHAIN

How does a bicycle work?

Between the two large wheels of a bicycle is a much smaller wheel with little teeth on it. This small wheel is called a sprocket. The foot pedals are attached to this sprocket. When a rider pushes the foot pedals, the sprocket turns. One end of a chain is looped around the sprocket. The other end fits around a smaller sprocket in the center of the bicycle's rear wheel. When the large sprocket turns, so does the chain. It turns the small sprocket and the large rear wheel. The bicycle moves forward.

How fast do bicycles go?

The average bike rider can cycle 12 miles an hour. Racers reach 60 miles an hour and more. The fastest bike ride on record was John Howard's 1985 trek across some Utah salt flats. He reached 152 miles an hour!

One man balanced on a bike for 5 hours and 25 minutes —staying absolutely still!

BIKES FOR KIDS

What is a tricycle?

A tricycle is a vehicle with pedals, a steering bar, and three wheels. Most tricycles are low so that young children can climb on easily. Since it has three wheels, a tricycle usually doesn't tip over, so the rider doesn't have to worry about falling. The rider can just climb on, pedal, and have fun!

Training wheels help this rider keep her bike balanced.

Why do people put training wheels on the backs of bikes?

Training wheels keep a bicycle steady and upright. We put them on a bike to help the rider learn how to keep the bike balanced.

A bicycle tips over when it's standing still. It tips over easily when moving slowly, too. It's easier to keep a bike balanced and upright only when it is moving. Training wheels give the bike an extra support on each side. After the rider learns how to balance, the training wheels are taken off.

How do the training wheels work to balance the bicycle?

Try this experiment to see why training wheels work. Stand up straight with your feet close together. Ask someone— someone you trust!—to give you a gentle push sideways. With your feet close together, it's easy to fall over. You probably have to take a step to keep from falling. Now stand with your feet about as far apart as your shoulders. Ask the person to give you another gentle push. This time it is much easier to keep from falling over. With your feet farther apart, you are more stable because you have a wider base. The bicycle is the same. Without training wheels, it tips over easily. But when you attach training wheels to it, you make its base much wider.

21

UNUSUAL CYCLES

What was the longest bicycle ever built?

You've probably heard of a bicycle built for 2. Well, the longest bicycle was built for 35! Made in Belgium, it was taken for a test ride in 1979. The bike weighed more than a ton and was more than 66 feet long. That's longer than ten regular bicycles placed end to end.

This is a bicycle built for 21 people.

What was the smallest bicycle ever built?

The world's smallest ridable bicycle has wheels just over two inches high. Weighing only two pounds, it's so small that it fits in the palm of a man's hand! This tiny bike has wheels made of gold, and diamonds on its pedals. Its owner Charly Charles rides it in Las Vegas, Nevada.

Are there cycles with only one wheel?

Yes, there are. They're called unicycles—meaning that they have one wheel. They're very hard to ride. It takes a lot of practice to learn how to balance on them. You've probably seen circus performers riding unicycles.

22

What is a mountain bike?

A mountain bike, or all-terrain bike, is a sturdy, heavy bicycle that people started using in the 1980s. The tires of mountain bikes are slightly larger than those on normal bicycles. These bikes are supertough and built to last. Riders take mountain bikes over rough ground and on forest trails where normal bikes might get damaged.

Here's the start of an exciting bicycle motocross!

What is a bicycle motocross?

A bicycle motocross is a type of bike race held outdoors over rugged terrain. The riders use small but tough bicycles to jump over obstacles, climb hills, and weave through moguls (MO-gulls), which are bumps in the ground.

CYCLES WITH ENGINES

What is a motorcycle?

A motorcycle is a two- or three-wheeled vehicle powered by a gasoline engine. Some motorcycles have no engine cover, so the engine is visible between the two wheels.

What is a dirt bike?

A dirt bike is a motorized bike that has a supertough frame and large tires with a wide tread. True to its name, a dirt bike can ride over dirt, mud, and sand. The fenders of a dirt bike are extra high and extra wide. These help protect the driver from the mud and dirt kicked up by the spinning tires. Dirt bikes can be dangerous and cause bad falls. Riders must wear special clothes to protect themselves from injury.

ALL-TERRAIN VEHICLE

What is an ATV?

The letters ATV stand for All-Terrain Vehicle. That means it can ride over rugged land, through the woods, or on a sandy beach. ATVs have four wheels and powerful engines. Since ATVs are very dangerous vehicles, they need expert handling. They should be used only by experienced adults.

24

CHAPTER 3

ALL ABOARD!

Pack your suitcase, buy your ticket, and hop aboard the Snoopy Express. We're off to see old-time trains and modern ones, too. Be sure not even to blink because you might miss the really fast ones. Do you hear the whistle? All aboard!

THE FIRST TRAINS

When did people first start using trains?

The very first trains were used by miners before 1600. These trains had no motors, and they weren't pulled by animals. They were simple wooden tubs that the miners pushed along wooden rails. Later, miners used horses for pulling wagons along the tracks.

Why do trains run on rails?

A vehicle running on rails doesn't hit holes, ruts, mud, or bumps as a car or a wagon on the road does. Pulling a car on rails is easier than pulling a car of the same weight along a road. When a car runs on rails, there is less friction (FRICK-shun), or rubbing, to slow the wheels. So they roll faster and more freely.

YOU HAVE TO PUT THE TRAIN ON THE TRACK IF YOU WANT IT TO RUN.

When was the first railroad built?

The first public railroad was built in England in 1825. It ran along 20 miles of metal tracks. At first the plan was to have horses pull the trains, but the railroad company decided to use steam engines instead. Each steam engine was able to pull a much heavier load than horses would have been able to pull. Because of its powerful engines, the railroad was a great success.

In the United States, the first railroad service began in 1828, using horse-drawn cars. Before too long, however, the American railroad companies switched to steam power.

How fast were the first railroad trains?

In 1830, a British steam locomotive named *Rocket* reached a speed of 29 miles an hour. People thought that the *Rocket* was very fast, and it *was* in those days. Back then the average train moved at a speed of 15 miles an hour.

How did the first trains in America look?

In the 1830s, America's first steam-powered trains were pulled by a car with a steam boiler, a round furnace with a smokestack in the center. Passengers sat in cars shaped like stagecoaches. These coaches were mounted on flat platforms with wheels.

One early train used a sail. The wind moved the train along the rails!

TODAY'S RAILROAD CARS— FROM THE COWCATCHER TO THE CABOOSE

What is a cowcatcher?

A cowcatcher is the iron grill at the front of the first car of a train. The cowcatcher sweeps over the tracks. Its name came from what it was used for—pushing stray cows from the tracks in front of the train.

What is a locomotive?

A locomotive is the railroad car that holds the train's engine. Usually, the locomotive is at the front of a train and pulls it. Sometimes, it is at the back of a train and pushes it instead. People often use the word *locomotive* to mean the engine itself.

The Trans-Siberian Railroad in Russia is the largest railroad system in the world. Its tracks would stretch from New York to California—and back again!

Why do locomotive engineers use train whistles?

Locomotive engineers use whistles to warn people and animals that a train is coming. They also use train whistles to signal crew members and other railroad workers. "Whistle talk" is a code made up of short and long toots. For example, one short toot means stop. Two long toots means go.

What other safety measures do locomotive engineers depend on to prevent accidents?

Railroads have other safety measures besides train-whistle warnings. One of these is the block signal system. A block is a length of railroad track, usually one or two miles long. To prevent collisions, only one train at a time is allowed in a block. Colored lights signal whether a train may enter a block. Red means stop. Green means go. Yellow means go ahead with caution. Some block signals are hand-operated by railroad people along the line. Other block signals are operated by computers.

Some locomotives have special panels with signals that give the same information as the signal lights on the tracks. If an engineer does not notice a panel signal to stop, the train will stop automatically. Crew members also use two-way radios to speak with faraway stations and train yards. This allows them to warn the train's conductor if there is danger ahead.

What is a Pullman car?

A Pullman car—sometimes called a sleeper car—is a train car with a place for sleeping. The Pullman car was named after George Pullman, one of the first Americans to make train travel more comfortable for passengers. If you had ridden on one of the first Pullman trains, you would have eaten fancy foods beneath the light of crystal chandeliers!

What is a caboose?

The last car of a train is often called the caboose. Long ago it was reserved for the trainmen or owners of cattle. Today the caboose often carries passengers and cargo, just like the other cars of the train.

FREIGHT TRAINS

What is a freight train?

A freight train doesn't carry passengers. It moves packages, metal, animals, mail, lumber, and other goods from place to place. An average freight train has about 100 cars.

What's the longest freight train on record?

The longest freight train stretched 4 miles. It was made up of 500 coal cars and 6 diesel locomotives—3 at the front and 3 near the middle of the train. Weighing 47,000 tons, this freight train traveled 157 miles on the Norfolk and Western Railway on November 15, 1967.

What types of cars do you find in a freight train?

Freight trains have different kinds of cars to carry different kinds of freight. For example, boxcars carry grain, cans, and packages. Boxcars are enclosed. Flatcars are open platforms used for carrying logs, steel, and machinery. Stockcars carry cattle, pigs, or sheep, so the cars have open slats for the animals to breathe. There are also refrigerator cars for fruits and vegetables, tank cars for oil and milk—and even poultry cars for chickens!

TUNNELS AND UNDERGROUND TRAINS

Why are railroad tunnels built?

Most railroad tunnels are built through hills and mountains. Instead of winding miles and miles of track around a mountain, builders usually cut through the mountain in a straight line. With the help of a tunnel, the train route is shorter— and safer, too!

How is a railroad tunnel built?

It takes a special crew of engineers and experts to build a railroad tunnel. Workers drill holes deep into the side of a hill or a mountain. They pack an explosive such as dynamite into the holes. Huge sections of rock and earth are blasted away in seconds. The workers clear away the loose rock from the explosion, then they drill more holes.

After they have cleared the tunnel all the way through, they line it with concrete. Then they lay down the track. Finally, the railroad tunnel is ready to be used.

31

What is a subway?

A subway is a passenger railroad that runs mostly underground. It is powered by electricity. Because it is underground, a subway is perfect for a crowded city. Except for its station entrances, it does not take up any street space. Since subways carry people all around a city, the trains make lots of stops along their routes.

The Tokyo, Japan, subway system hires special workers to squeeze passengers into crowded trains! They wear special uniforms and clean white gloves. Despite their job, the "squeezers" are very polite.

KINDLY, STEP IN, PLEASE.

When was the first city subway opened?

The first subway was opened in London, England, on January 10, 1863. The trains used steam locomotives that burned a type of fuel called coke. The subway smelled so bad, it was nicknamed "the sewer"! The tunnels were so dirty and dark that some passengers carried candles to light their way. But people still used these trains. This first subway carried nearly 10 million passengers in its first year.

How many cities in the world have subways?

There are about 70 subway systems in the world today. Some of the cities with large subway systems are New York, Paris, London, Berlin, Moscow, Hamburg, Tokyo, and Boston. Not all cities call them subways. Some use the name metro, underground, or tube.

The busiest subway system in the world is in Moscow. It may carry 6½ million passengers a day!

33

STREETCARS, CABLE CARS, AND MONORAILS

What is a streetcar?

A streetcar is a vehicle that moves along rails that are set into the surface of the road. Streetcars usually run within city limits.

How were the first streetcars pulled?

In the early years of the twentieth century, streetcars were pulled by horses. The rails made the horses' task easier. At the same time, the passengers got a better ride since the tracks were smoother than the bumpy roads.

How do modern streetcars get their power?

Modern streetcars get their power from electricity. Today there are two kinds of streetcars. One is called a trolley car. Its power comes from an overhead electric line. The other is called a cable car. It is pulled by a heavy steel rope called a cable. The cable moves along a slot under the surface of the street.

How are cable cars used?

Cable cars are used to climb steep hills and mountains. In San Francisco, the hills are so steep that buses and trolleys have trouble climbing them. Cable cars do the job.

Canadians use this monorail to get around in Vancouver.

What is a monorail?

A monorail is a railroad that has only one rail. This rail may be above or below the monorail cars. Monorails cannot travel as fast as other trains, but they are cheaper, cleaner, and quieter to run.

TODAY'S SUPER TRAINS

How fast are modern trains?

The average modern train travels at about 65 miles an hour. However, many passenger trains today speed along at 90 miles an hour.

How do modern trains run?

Most modern trains are pulled by locomotives that use diesel-electric engines. A diesel-electric engine is similar to a gasoline engine, but it burns diesel fuel, a kind of oil, instead of gasoline. The diesel turns generators, which supply electrical energy to the electric motors. The motors then turn the locomotive's wheels.

Some locomotives are fully electric. They use no oil. They get electric current from wires hung above the railroad track or from a third rail that runs on the ground inside the track. As with the diesel engine, the electric power turns the train's wheels.

The world's fastest speed for a passenger train was 252 miles an hour, recorded in West Germany in May, 1988!

A MAGLEV DOGHOUSE?

What is the bullet train?

The bullet train is a super-fast electric train in Japan. Called the shinkansen (SHIN-kan-SEN) by the Japanese, it cruises at 130 miles per hour! When two bullet trains pass each other at such a high speed, the air between them is put under great pressure. This causes a loud booming sound. Since the trains have special seals on the doors, passengers don't hear the noise. The bullet train, which carries 100,000 passengers a day, has been running since 1964.

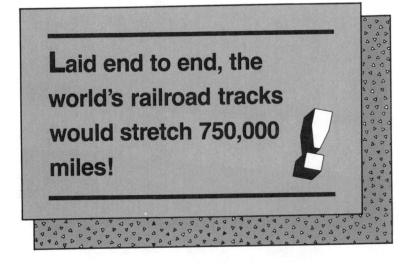

Laid end to end, the world's railroad tracks would stretch 750,000 miles!

What is a TGV?

The TGV is an electrical train in France that's the fastest thing on rails. TGV stands for a French phrase for "very great speed"—and that's what makes this train famous. On a normal day, the TGV zips along at a speed of 170 miles an hour, but, in 1990, it went as fast as 320 miles an hour!

What does *maglev* mean?

Maglev stands for "magnetic levitation." This is a new way to move trains by using electric motors and magnets. The powerful force of the magnets actually lifts the vehicle into the air! Engineers think a maglev train could probably travel as fast as 500 miles an hour.

Maglev trains are not running yet, but scientists in Japan and Germany are working hard on new designs for this speedy train.

FRENCH TGV TRAIN

Trains made it possible to travel long distances, but they could go only to places where tracks had been built. People were still pulling their carriages and carts with horses, oxen, or donkeys to get to places where trains didn't go. It was pretty hard work—until the automobile came along!

START YOUR ENGINE!

THE FIRST AUTOMOBILES

Who invented the first successful automobile?

EARLY CAR

The first successful automobile was invented in 1770 by a French engineer named Nicolas Joseph Cugnot (KYOU-no). It rode on three wheels and was used to move guns from place to place.

In 1801, Richard Trevithick (trev-EE-thik) built the first automobile to carry passengers.

What kind of engine did the first automobile use?

It used a steam engine. Coal was fired up to boil water and turn it into steam. Inside the engine was a piece of metal called a piston. The steam pushed the piston back and forth. The piston turned a metal rod connected to the car's wheels. When the rod moved, the wheels moved—and so did the car.

Why didn't steam-driven cars last?

NOW I'M REALLY STEAMED!

Most people didn't like steam-driven cars. They filled the air with smoke wherever they went, and hot coals sometimes shot out of the engines! The cars moved slowly—only 10 to 15 miles an hour—but they were so noisy that they frightened both horses and people. In addition, stagecoach and railroad companies did not like the new automobiles. They were afraid that if many people rode in these cars, fewer passengers would ride on their lines. In England, laws limited the use of steam-driven cars. For example, one 1865 law said that a signalman had to walk in front of each car and warn people it was coming!

What does *horsepower* mean?

Horsepower is an old English way of measuring an engine's power to do a certain amount of work in a certain period of time. An engine's horsepower compares it to the number of horses it would take to do the work in the same amount of time.

Who are the "fathers" of the modern automobile?

Gottlieb Daimler and Karl Benz, both German, are considered the fathers of the modern automobile. Working separately, Benz (in 1885) and Daimler (in 1886) developed gasoline engines that worked much like the engines used in cars today. Daimler put his engine into a motorcycle. Benz's engine powered a three-wheeled automobile. The company Karl Benz started is now called Mercedes-Benz.

What was an electric car?

An electric car was an automobile powered by one or more electric motors. The motor got its power from a battery. The battery had to be plugged into a wall socket from time to time to be recharged.

Electric cars were popular in the 1890s and early 1900s. They were clean and quiet and reached speeds up to 20 miles an hour. However, after an electric car had traveled only about 50 miles, the battery died! Today, new technology has made them easier to use and, by 1998, there may be 40,000 electric cars produced every year!

In 1896, the automobile was so new and strange, it was shown in Barnum and Bailey's Circus!

HENRY FORD AND THE MODEL T

Who was Henry Ford?

Henry Ford was an American pioneer in the building of cars. In 1913, he introduced the moving automobile assembly line. Each worker on an assembly line did just one small job in putting a car together. The parts were on a moving belt. When a worker finished his or her job, the parts moved along to the next worker.

Before Ford's method, workers spent a lot of time doing complicated jobs, but with the assembly line, factories were able to produce cars more quickly and cheaply than before. Ford sold his cars for less than other carmakers, so more people could afford to own them. Because of Henry Ford, cars became a part of American life.

MODEL T FORD

What was the Model T?

The Model T was Ford's most famous car. The Ford Motor Company built this model between 1908 and 1927. To keep prices down, Ford made only small changes in the Model T each year, and he built the car in only one color—black.

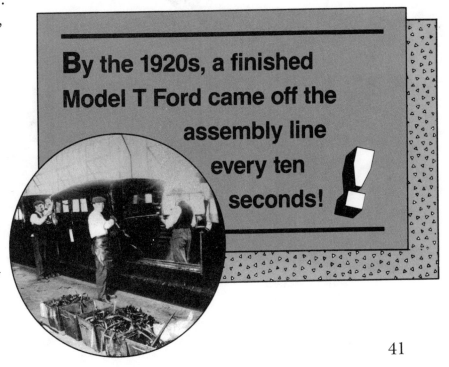

By the 1920s, a finished Model T Ford came off the assembly line every ten seconds!

41

THE GAS ENGINE

How do the engines of our cars work?

When the engine is turned on, gasoline goes to a part of the engine called the carburetor (CAR-buh-ray-tur). There, the gasoline mixes with air. The gas and air mixture moves to the cylinders (SILL-in-durz). These cylinders are hollow spaces inside a solid block of metal.

Inside each cylinder is a piston, a solid piece of metal that moves up and down. The piston moves down to suck in the gasoline and air mixture. Then it moves up again. Just as the piston gets near the top of the cylinder, a spark plug gives off an electric spark. This causes the mixture to explode. Pressure from the explosion pushes the piston down again. This happens in one cylinder after another. These tiny explosions create the energy to move the car.

Can automobile engines run on other fuels?

Yes. Many trucks run on diesel fuel, which is made from petroleum. Engines have to be specially built to burn diesel fuel, and the fuel leaves a dirty residue after it is burned. Another fuel that a car can use is methanol. Methanol is made from grain, and it is used to fuel racing cars. There is also gasohol, a mixture of gasoline and alcohol. Gasohol burns more cleanly than plain gasoline, but it is expensive to produce. Engineers are looking for a cheaper, cleaner fuel for cars of the future.

RULES OF THE ROAD

CAR STEERING WHEEL AND DASHBOARD

How does a driver control a car on the road?

A driver uses the steering wheel to direct the car, and pedals to control the car's speed. One of these pedals, the gas pedal, is connected to the engine. When the driver pushes the gas pedal with his or her foot, the car moves. Pushing the other pedal, the brake pedal, makes the car stop.

The car's lights, heater, windshield wipers, air conditioner, and radio are usually controlled by levers, knobs, or buttons on the dashboard. The dashboard is the long panel inside the car just ahead of the steering wheel. The dashboard also has numbers or dials that light up. They tell a driver how much gas and oil are in the car, and how fast the driver is going.

Why do cars have license plates?

All states require car owners to register their cars. License plates are part of this registration. A license plate can help the police find a stolen car. It can also help identify a car in case of an accident.

States also use car registrations as a way to check the safety of automobiles. Some states require car owners to have their cars checked once or twice a year. Unless the car meets the state's safety standards, the owner cannot renew the car's registration.

Why do you need seat belts and shoulder harnesses in a car?

Seat belts and shoulder harnesses help protect passengers from injury during an accident. They hold a person in place when a car suddenly stops or turns. Seat belts and shoulder harnesses often save lives. Expert drivers use seat belts—and you should always wear yours, too!

What does a speed limit on a road mean?

A speed limit is the fastest safe driving speed on a certain road. On most highways in the United States, the speed limit is 55 miles an hour. This limit is meant to save gasoline as well as lives. When automobiles move at higher speeds, they use more gasoline.

If a car goes over the speed limit, the driver may be stopped by a police officer and given a speeding ticket. The driver then has to pay a fine. If he or she gets too many speeding tickets, the state government will take away his or her driver's license.

Every year more than seven million cars end up in junkyards!

What makes police cars different?

Most cars driven by police officers have sirens and round or bar-shaped lights on the roof. When these are turned on, the noise and flashing lights warn people that the police are near. Other drivers slow down to let the police rush to the emergency.

Most police cars also have two-way radios. When someone needs help, the message comes over the radio to the police officer in the car. Some police cars also have computers. When the officer punches in a license plate number, the computer tells him or her who the car belongs to and if that person has any unpaid tickets. All these facts come from the computer in less than ten seconds!

Super Cars of Today and Tomorrow

What's new in the world of cars?

Since the time of the Model T, car owners have enjoyed automobiles with many new features. We can get air-conditioning, adjustable and heated seats, car phones, and gauges that show the outside temperature and which direction the car is traveling in. Some cars even talk to the driver! They tell the driver when a door is open, or when the car needs gas.

Engineers are working on a car that flashes information—right on the windshield. It can show a map of the car's destination and will even warn a driver if another car is too close!

Why are racing cars built differently?

Racing cars are built for speed and power. Many cars, like those driven in Grand Prix (grahn pree) races, have sleek bodies. They are built narrow and close to the ground. This is so the force of the wind coming at them won't slow them down. Instead, the wind streams over and around the car.

Some racing cars even have "wings" mounted on their backs. These wings, also called airfoils, are not meant to lift the cars off the ground. In fact, they do just the opposite. They push the cars closer to the road, which helps them go faster.

Racing cars also have wide tires, good for going around corners and giving the car stability.

What is stock car racing?

Stock car racing is the most popular motor sport in America. These racing cars look similar to cars driven on the street. Stock car racers start with showroom cars, which they rebuild. On the track, stock cars are awesome, mean-racing machines.

STOCK CAR

What are funny cars?

Funny cars are a type of drag-racing car. A drag race is a short-distance race at super speeds. A funny car's body looks like a regular street car, but it's really only a fiberglass copy. Funny cars have powerful engines built to get to super speeds fast. They race one-on-one, so you won't see more than two cars on the track at any one time.

FUNNY CAR

What are rocket cars?

Rocket cars are the fastest wheels on Earth! They are shaped like a rocket with small wheels underneath and larger wheels behind the rear fin. One of these supercars broke the sound barrier at more than 700 miles an hour! You can tell they are fast by their hot names—*Blue Flame*, *Spirit of America*, *Rocket*, and *Thrust 2*. How do they get their power? From built-in rockets and jets!

It took powerful brakes and a seven-foot parachute to stop the *Blue Flame* after its 630-mile-an-hour ride! Nine years later, in 1979, the *Rocket* broke the speed of sound at more than 739 miles an hour!

Are there cars that run on solar power?

Yes. One is called the Sunraycer and is powered by the heat of the sun! The Sunraycer looks like a blue bubble on four wheels. It's more than 20 feet long and 6 feet wide. Since a solar-powered car runs on sunlight, a rainy day could be a problem for it, but not this one! A battery inside the Sunraycer soaks up the sun's rays so that the car will move even on a cloudy day.

SUNRAYCER

47

BUSES AND BIG RIGS

What would we do without buses to take us to school, through the city—or even across the country? And the millions of trucks on our country's highways move just about anything you can imagine. There's no doubt about it. It takes big wheels to do big jobs!

BUS STOP

BUSES

Where does the word *bus* come from?

The word *bus* is short for *omnibus*, which means "for everyone."

What were early buses like?

The first buses were large carriages drawn by horses. One of the earliest buses carried people around Paris as long ago as 1662.

New York City started bus service in 1829 with its "sociable." The sociable was a carriage with enough room to seat ten passengers.

In the same year, the first omnibus rolled down the streets of London. The omnibus was pulled by three horses side by side. This caused terrible traffic jams. The streets weren't wide enough for the omnibus and other traffic, too. Later, these buses were made narrower so they could be pulled by two horses.

DOUBLE-DECKER BUS

Why was the double-decker bus invented?

The London omnibus was very popular. Many people wanted to ride it, but there was not enough room. So some people used to hold on to the roof. Because of this, a long bus seat was added to the roof in 1847. Seats on the open top were half price. Later, a canopy was added to protect passengers from rain and sun. Today double-decker buses run in London, but they have closed tops.

What are the longest buses in the world?

The longest buses in the world are each 76 feet long. That's twice as long as an average bus. These very long buses, used in the Middle East, have room enough to seat 121 people.

TRUCKS!

Why are there many different kinds of trucks?

Different kinds of trucks are needed to do many different kinds of jobs. Refrigerator trucks carry food that spoils if it is not kept cold. Tank trucks carry liquids such as gasoline. Small enclosed trucks called panel trucks carry small packages and mail over short distances. And bottle trucks have special racks for holding cases of bottles.

Here's a big truck on the move.

What is a trailer?

A trailer is a van or wagon that is pulled by another vehicle. It has no engine of its own. Some trailers are boxcars built to carry everything from clothes to furniture. Some trailers are called flatbeds. They are open platforms used to carry heavy machines—or other trucks.

The first postal trucks in the United States were made so that a mule could be hitched to one if the steam engine failed to work!

50

What is a tractor truck?

A tractor truck, or "rig," is the front part of a big tractor-trailer. It contains the engine and the cab, where the driver sits. The tractor truck can be driven without the trailer, but the trailer can't be driven without the tractor truck because it has no engine of its own. Power for the trailer's brakes and lights comes from the tractor truck.

TRACTOR TRAILER

Are there any other kinds of trailers?

Yes. Some mobile homes are trailers that can be pulled by a car or a truck. Mobile homes are out-fitted with beds, seats, and even bathrooms and kitchens. Many people spend their vacations traveling around in trailers. Some people build foundations under their trailers and live in them all the time.

In 1904, there were only 700 trucks being used in the United States. Today, there are more than 12 million trucks on the road in the United States!

CAMP GROUNDS

BULLDOZERS, DUMP TRUCKS, CRANES, AND CEMENT MIXERS

What is a bulldozer?

A bulldozer, or earth mover, is used to clear away trees and spread dirt. This big machine has a giant blade or shovel in front. A bulldozer runs on belts of metal tracks instead of wheels. The tracks spread the weight of the bulldozer over a greater area and keep the machine from sinking into soft ground. Because the tracks are rigid, the bulldozers can ride over rough surfaces easily.

DUMP TRUCK

What are dump trucks and cranes?

Wherever people are building houses or highways, you'll find unusual trucks on the job. Dump trucks have a special open box on the back that tilts so that gravel and dirt can be poured out of it. Cranes also are used at most building sites. A crane has a long arm able to lift heavy objects. Cranes run on long, flat belts, called tracks, rather than on tires. That way they don't get stuck in mud or gravel.

What are cement mixers?

Cement mixers are trucks that carry a giant barrel filled with cement. This barrel rotates on the back of the truck. The cement is poured through a narrow chute.

52

FIRE ENGINES AND AMBULANCES

What were the first fire trucks like?

The first fire trucks were just water pumps on wheels. These pumps were pulled to fires by horses or men. In the early 1800s, American fire companies used steam engines pulled by men or horses. Fire companies tried to outdo one another by hiring artists to paint beautiful scenes on the sides of their engines. They gave the engines fancy names such as *Live Oak* and *Ocean Wave*.

Fire horses of the early 1900s were well trained. As soon as the fire alarm rang, the horses trotted out from their stalls by themselves and stood ready in front of the fire trucks!

What is an engine truck?

When the fire alarm sounds today, fire trucks rush to the scene. One type of fire truck, the engine truck, arrives with its own booster tank of water. This water will be used if the fire fighters can't hook up their hoses to a hydrant (HIGH-drant), a water pipe on the sidewalk, or to a stand-pipe, a large faucet on the outside of some buildings.

What is a superpumper?

A superpumper is a mighty rig with the power to shoot water as far as 1,000 feet away. It can even reach fires in skyscrapers! With a superpumper's help, fire fighters don't have to get close to a fire to put it out.

53

Which fire truck carries the ladders?

A ladder truck, or aerial (AIR-ee-al) truck, carries ladders that work electrically. This special equipment helps fire fighters reach rooftops and upper stories of buildings to put out fires and rescue people. The ladders are 100 feet long and can reach up to the tenth story of a building. Many lives have been saved with the aerial ladder and with the cherry picker.

What is a cherry picker?

A cherry picker is a traveling crane. It has an arm about 75 feet long, with a big metal bucket on the end of the arm. The cherry picker's bucket carries fire fighters up to rooftops or high windows. Sometimes people trapped in burning buildings climb out of windows and into the big bucket. The crane then lowers them to the ground, where they can climb out to safety.

Fire fighters also use the cherry picker to put out fires in very old buildings. If there is a chance the old building will fall down, the fire fighters spray the fire from the bucket of the cherry picker. This way, if the building collapses, the fire fighters will be safe in the cherry picker.

What were the first ambulances like?

The first ambulances were probably horse-drawn carts. The Spanish army used them as long ago as 1487 to carry its wounded off the battlefield. Before that, armies probably used litters and stretchers to carry wounded soldiers.

What are modern ambulances like?

Most modern ambulances are about the size of vans or small trucks. Inside, they are like traveling hospitals. Ambulances carry medical equipment to treat people who are sick or have had an accident. Specially trained people ride in ambulances to care for the patients during the trip to the hospital.

AMBULANCE

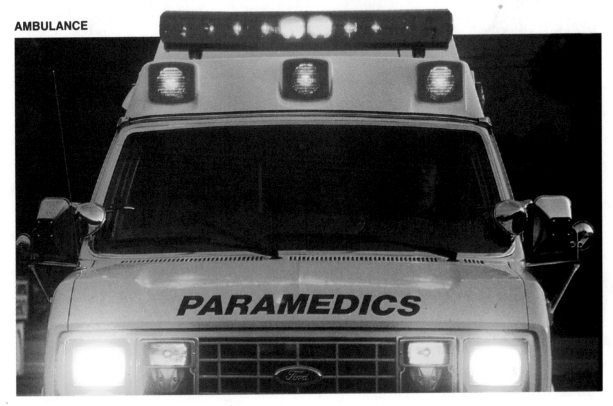

DID YOU KNOW...?

ARMY PORTABLE BRIDGE

● When an army needs to get across a river quickly, there's only one way to go—on a portable bridge! Although this vehicle looks like a tank when it's traveling, it's really an instant bridge. Its platform can unfold to span a 60-foot river. After the soldiers and equipment have gone over it, the instant bridge folds up and moves on again—until the next river!

● What's that in the sky? Not a bird—but an amazing flying car! For years inventors dreamed of a vehicle that would grip the road, then take to the air over traffic jams. Some of these flying cars were actually made and some really worked—but not very well. That's because planes need to be lightweight to work well, and cars need to be heavy to do their job on the road.

● Escalators are moving stairways. The first escalator was introduced in Paris in 1900. Today, the longest escalator, in St. Petersburg, Russia, has 729 steps!

I SEE YOU RAN INTO ANOTHER FLYING CAR...

- Some sidewalks move. They are really belts of rubber that carry people along flat surfaces or up slight slopes. These sidewalks help the flow of crowds through long airport or museum corridors, and they sure beat walking!

- Imagine a dump truck that can carry a load weighing as much as 88 cars—or 2,000 people! One monster-sized dump truck can do just that!

And what does this mountain-mover look like? It's as tall as a medium tree and as wide as three Cadillacs—and it's thirsty. It takes 500 gallons of gas to fill up its huge tank!

- Big 18-wheeled tractor-trailers usually zoom along superhighways, but the trailers can also ride "piggyback" aboard railroad flatcars. Traveling this way, the trailers can go long distances without tying up the highways or using gasoline!

- Early elevators were powered by steam engines or pressure from water or oil. Today most elevators are run by electricity—and they can give you a pretty fast lift! The elevators in Tokyo's Sunshine 60 building travel upward at more than 20 miles an hour!

GOING UP?

When you live near water, there's only one way to travel across it and stay dry—in a boat! Boats can cut through an ocean's high waves or skim across a calm lake. No matter how big or small your boat is, though, one thing is certain—it had better float!

ROW, ROW, ROW YOUR BOAT

CHAPTER 6

WHY BOATS FLOAT

What makes a boat float?

When something solid, such as a boat, is put into a liquid, such as water, the solid pushes some of the liquid aside. If the solid weighs more than the liquid it pushes aside, it will sink. If it weighs less, it will float. A huge, heavy ship floats even though it is made of steel. Because it contains a lot of air, it weighs less than the water it pushes aside. That is why it floats.

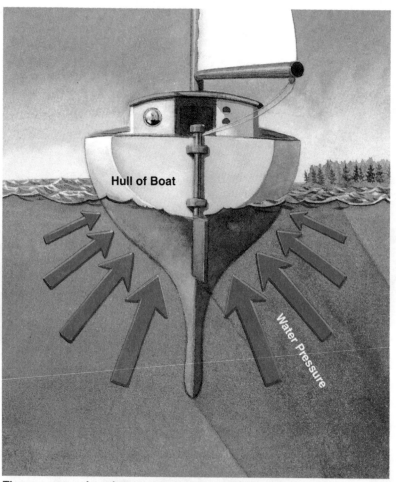

These arrows show how water presses against a hull to make a boat float.

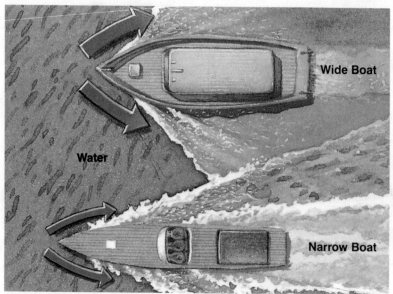

Narrow boats move through water more quickly than wide boats because they have less water to push aside.

Why are most boats long and narrow?

Long, narrow boats can go through the water quickly. A force called "drag" holds back anything that moves through water. The wider the boat, the more drag there is, so a narrow boat can go faster than a wide one.

THE FIRST RAFTS

How did people first cross rivers and streams?

If the water was too deep to walk through, people probably swam, but only the strongest swimmers could have gotten across a wide river. Some early, tired swimmer probably grabbed onto a floating log. He or she became the first person to use a raft—a simple platform that floats on water.

What were early rafts like?

Once people realized that they could float on a log, they probably tied two logs together and then three logs and then four logs for bigger and bigger rafts. Soon people began to experiment with other types of rafts. In Egypt, for example, they tied together bundles of sticks or heavy reeds.

The earliest rafts were probably made of wood, much like this river craft.

How did people move their rafts?

At first, the raft rider had nothing to paddle with but his or her hands. Later, riders probably used a stick to push the raft through the water. Still later, people discovered that a flat piece of wood worked better than a stick. It made the raft go faster. That's how the paddle was invented.

Are there any famous rafts?

The *Kon-Tiki* is one of the most famous rafts in the world. It was built in 1947 by Thor Heyerdahl (HI-ur-doll), a Norwegian scientist. Heyerdahl sailed the tiny *Kon-Tiki* thousands of miles across the Pacific Ocean without any modern equipment. He went from South America to Polynesia (pol-uh-NEE-zhuh)— a group of islands south of Hawaii. Heyerdahl's voyage proved that people could have made the same trip by raft 1,500 years ago. It is possible, then, that the people of Polynesia are the great-, great-, great-grandchildren of South American Indians.

What did the *Kon-Tiki* look like?

The *Kon-Tiki* was a copy of the rafts used by natives of the South Pacific. It was made of balsa, a light wood that floats easily. It was 45 feet long and 18 feet wide. On the center of the raft was a bamboo cabin that Heyerdahl used for shelter.

The *Kon-Tiki* flew flags from several different nations, including the United States.

What were the first boats like?

The first boats developed from rafts. To keep dry, people turned up the sides of their reed rafts. In this way, they invented a boat that looked like a saucer, but these round boats were hard to steer. It didn't take long for people to learn to build longer, thinner boats. These were easier to steer and could move through the water much faster.

CANOES

What is a canoe?

A canoe is a long, narrow boat that is pointed at both ends. One, two, or three people sit in the canoe, facing the front, or bow (rhymes with *cow*). They use a paddle, or paddles, to move the canoe through the water and to steer it. Canoes were among the first kinds of small boats.

What did the earliest Americans use when they traveled by water?

Native Americans used canoes. They had two kinds, dugout and birchbark, depending on where they lived. In the north, where birch trees grew, Native Americans made birchbark canoes. In other places, they made dugouts.

How did the Native Americans make a dugout canoe?

A dugout canoe was made from a long, thick log. The canoe maker burned the middle of the log in order to make the wood soft, but had to be careful not to burn all the way through. Then the canoe maker scraped, or dug out, all the soft, burned wood to make the inside hollow.

Dugout canoes are very strong but slow. They're also heavy—too heavy to be carried far on land.

MOVE IT... MOVE IT. WHAT'S WRONG HERE?

WE ALL STEP TO THE SOUND OF A DIFFERENT DRUMMER.

What is a birchbark canoe?

A birchbark canoe is much lighter than a dugout canoe. It can be carried easily from one stream to another. These canoes are made from strips of bark peeled from birch trees. After building a frame out of wood, the canoe maker sews the strips together, using tree roots for thread. Then the canoe maker attaches the bark to the canoe's wooden frame.

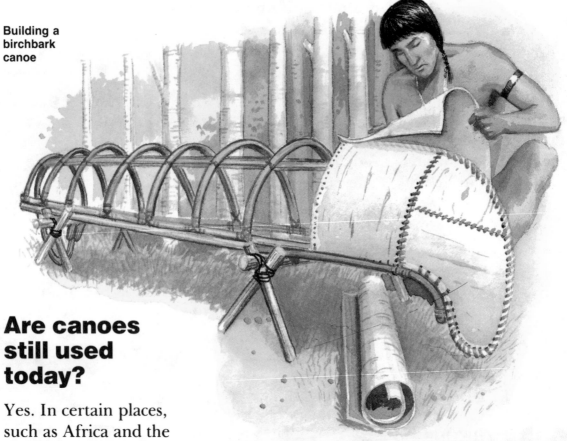

Building a birchbark canoe

Are canoes still used today?

Yes. In certain places, such as Africa and the South Pacific Islands, people still travel by canoe. In most other parts of the world, however, canoes are used mainly for fun. People take them on fishing or camping trips. Today, most canoes are built by machine, and they are made of canvas, light metal, or plastic.

In 1928, a man crossed the Atlantic Ocean in a canoe with a sail. The trip took 58 days!

KAYAKS AND ROWBOATS

What is a kayak?

A kayak (KI-ak) is the canoe the Eskimos have been using for thousands of years. It is long and pointed like most canoes.

Kayaks weigh very little. Because they are so light, they move quickly through the water.

Kayaks, however, are not open. Their top is covered, except for one small hole for the paddler. Most kayaks have room for only one paddler.

Some kayak paddles look like canoe paddles, but most are double-bladed, that is, they have a blade at each end. The paddler dips one blade into the water on the right side, then swings the paddle over and dips the other blade in on the left side.

How are kayaks made?

Kayaks are made in almost the same way as birchbark canoes. The Eskimos just use different materials. The frame of the kayak is made of wood or whalebone—the tough plates whales have instead of teeth. Sealskin is used for the outside. It is stretched tightly over the frame, leaving a small opening for the paddler.

Are kayaks always made of sealskin?

No. These days, most kayaks are made of light metal, wood, or plastic, just like canoes. Some kayaks and other small boats are made of heavy cloth that has rubber on one side. They must be pumped full of air, or inflated, before they will float. When there is no air in them, they can be folded up and stored in very small places. Kayaks and rubber rafts are used mostly for fun.

What is a rowboat?

A rowboat is any kind of boat that is moved by oars. An oar is longer than a paddle, but it's used the same way. The rower usually uses two oars, one on each side of the boat. To keep the oars from slipping into the water, they are held in place by oarlocks on the sides of the boat.

Rowboats tied to a dock

Did boats ever have more than two oars?

Yes. When people started building large ships, they needed many oars to move them. A galley, one of the earliest ships, sometimes had 50 or more oars.

Galleys were first used by the people who lived around the Mediterranean (med-ih-tuh-RAY-nee-un) Sea more than 3,000 years ago. Many of these people were from Egypt and Phoenicia (foh-NISH-uh), the land where Syria, Lebanon, and Israel are today.

Galleys were rowed by slaves who sat on benches. Each man held an oar with both hands. All the slaves rowed at once, to the beat of a drum. Most galleys also had one large oar at the back of the boat. It was used for steering.

EGYPTIAN GALLEY — STEERING OAR — CABIN — MAST FOR SAIL

What was the biggest galley ship?

The biggest galley ship was made in Alexandria, Egypt. It was 420 feet long and could carry 4,000 rowers. Eight men were needed to handle each 57-foot oar. Built more than 2,000 years ago, this giant galley was the largest ship to be powered by humans.

Early Romans believed that ships needed eyes to see. So they painted eyes on their galleys!

What's the difference between boats and ships?

Boats are smaller than ships, and they rarely travel far out on the ocean. Ships do. They are large, seagoing vessels. Ships are used for trading, carrying passengers, and fighting battles.

CHAPTER 7

Captain Brown and his merry crew are here to take you on a super sailboat journey. If we catch the wind just right, there'll be smooth sailing ahead! You won't need a paddle or an engine—just a tall sail and the mighty wind. Let's go!

CATCHING THE WIND

EARLY SAILBOATS

Why did people add sails to their boats?

A sail on a boat can catch the wind. This, in turn, causes the boat to move. The ancient Egyptians discovered this fact about 5,000 years ago. The first sails were made of thick materials that could trap the wind. Sailboat builders used a large piece of linen or papyrus (puh-PIE-russ)—a heavy, coarse paper.

The early sailors could travel only *with* the wind. If the wind was blowing in the wrong direction, they had to put down their sails and row the boat. It was not until the triangular sail was invented that sailing in almost any direction became possible. This happened about 1,600 years ago.

Who were the first sailors to use ships?

The Egyptians started to do a great deal of sailing more than 4,000 years ago. They made easy-to-sail ships from wooden boards. They sailed these ships around the Mediterranean, trading with other countries. Then, about 3,000 years ago, the Phoenicians began to design ships both for trading and for fighting sea battles. They made long, fast ships for fighting and short, wide ones for trading.

Were there galley ships with sails?

Although the first galleys had no sails, later ones did. Even so, their most important source of power was muscle. Sails helped the galleys move, but they still needed oars.

Who thought of using more than one sail?

About 2,500 years ago, both the Greeks and the Phoenicians came up with a new idea in ship design. Until then, ships had always had one mast—a pole for a sail—and one sail. The Greeks and Phoenicians added a second mast and two more sails. The new sails gave them extra speed and better control. About 2,000 years later, the Greeks added a third mast and a fourth sail.

THE VIKINGS

Who were the Vikings?

The Vikings were fierce seagoing pirates from Norway, Sweden, and Denmark. They raided Europe by sea about 1,000 years ago, and probably reached North America before Christopher Columbus did. The Vikings settled in areas that now are England, Russia, Iceland, and Greenland.

This painting shows Viking ships sailing through rough seas.

The Vikings founded the city of Dublin, Ireland!

What kind of ships did the Vikings use?

The Vikings used trading ships and warships. The trading ships were called *knorrs* (pronounce the *k*). The knorrs were very wide and carried goods for trading. They didn't have many oars, so there was a lot of room for cargo.

What were the warships like?

Viking warships were long, narrow, and fast. They had many oars and just one sail. The earliest of these were called long ships. Later, the Vikings built ships that were longer than the long ships! Each of these later ships had a wooden carving at the front. This carving, called a figurehead, was of a person or a monster, such as a dragon. Because the figurehead was often a dragon, the Vikings called these warships *drakkars*, which means "dragons."

Why did Vikings put figureheads on their ships?

Some figureheads served the same purpose as a name painted on a ship. They were used to identify the ship. The Vikings also believed figureheads scared away evil spirits. That's why carvings of dragon heads and monsters were common on Viking ships.

Why is the right side of a ship called starboard and the left called port?

The Vikings were the first to use those names. A typical Viking ship had a giant steering oar. It was on the right side, near the back of the ship. It was there for two reasons. First, most people are right-handed. Second, the ancient people believed that the right side of a ship was stronger than the left side. The right side of a Viking ship was eventually called the "steerboard." Over the years the word changed a little, to starboard.

Because the steering oar was in the way, the Vikings could not dock on the right side of the ship. They always docked with the left side facing port. So that's what they called it—and so do we.

EXPLORING WITH CHRISTOPHER COLUMBUS

Why did Columbus sail west to get to the East?

Christopher Columbus believed that the world was round. Before his time (the late 1400s), just about everyone had assumed that the world was flat. If the world really was round, Columbus thought, he should be able to reach the Indies—east of Europe—by sailing west. *The Indies* was a name for India, China, and the islands of Southeast Asia. In fact, Columbus believed the shortest route to be west across the Atlantic Ocean.

Columbus's biggest ship, the *Santa María*, probably looked like this.

When Columbus reached America for the first time, he thought he was in the Indies. That's why he named the people there Indians!

What kind of ships did Christopher Columbus use for his famous 1492 voyage?

Two of Columbus's ships, the *Niña* and the *Pinta*, were caravels. These light, fast sailing ships first became popular around 1400. They had three masts: the foremast (in the front), the mainmast (in the middle), and the mizzenmast (in the back). The foremast had a square sail. The other two masts had sails in the shape of triangles.

The third ship—and the largest—was a carrack. Known as the *Santa María*, it was the one Columbus himself traveled on. The ship had the same three masts as the caravels, but both the mainmast and the foremast had square sails. Only the mizzenmast had a sail in the shape of a triangle. A pole called a bowsprit stuck out from the front, or bow, of the ship. It held a small square sail.

FERDINAND MAGELLAN

Who was the first person to sail around the world?

Ferdinand Magellan always gets the credit, although he never actually completed the trip around the world. However, one of his ships did.

In 1519, Magellan decided to try to find a short route to the Indies. He planned to go around the tip of South America and then west to Asia.

Magellan left Spain with five ships. In two years, he got halfway around the world, but during the voyage, he was killed on a Pacific island. Of his five ships, four didn't complete the trip. One ship was wrecked on a rock. One returned to Spain early. One was left, leaking badly, on a Pacific island. One was lost. Only one ship completed the trip.

Where did Columbus's crew sleep?

On the floor! Only the most important officers of the *Niña*, the *Pinta*, and the *Santa María* slept in bunks. The other men slept on deck. However, after the first voyage to America, the crew slept below deck in hammocks. The hammock was a Native American invention that Columbus's men adopted.

WELL, HE ALMOST MADE IT!

THE SPANISH ARMADA

What was the Spanish Armada?

For many years, no country was as mighty as Spain when it came to ocean travel. During the 1500s, Spain had the largest fleet of ships in Europe. The fleet was known as the Spanish Armada. These ships were used by Spanish explorers to sail across the Atlantic Ocean to America. The Spaniards brought back many treasures from the New World, making Spain very rich.

The Armada also protected Spain from enemies and fought her battles when it was necessary. Because of its Armada, Spain was, for many years, one of the most powerful countries in Europe. In 1588, however, a fleet of English ships defeated the Armada. England became mistress of the sea.

The mighty Spanish Armada included 130 ships of war, 8,000 sailors, and 20,000 soldiers!

What is a galleon?

A galleon is a large wooden sailing ship that was popular in Europe during the mid-1500s. It was used for trading and, in wartime, for battle. A galleon was better for long-distance sea voyages than earlier ships. It was deeper, so it had bunk space for the whole crew.

The foremast and the mainmast of a galleon each had two or three sails. Sometimes the mizzenmast had two sails, also. Some of the early galleons had oars as well as sails, but galleons could be rowed only in smooth waters.

AREN'T THERE FOUR QUARTS TO A GALLEON, MA'AM?

GALLEON

THE MAYFLOWER

What kind of ship was the *Mayflower*?

The ship that carried the Pilgrims to the New World in 1620 was a fairly small trading ship. She was about 90 feet—as long as six cars lined up in a row. Some passengers on the *Mayflower* slept in bunks along the sides of the ship. Others made their beds on the floor of the covered deck. The upper part of the ship leaked, so the Pilgrims often felt ice-cold water splashing on them.

Before she carried passengers, the *Mayflower* had carried wine. Because of that, the ship's hold—the place where the cargo is kept—smelled quite sweet. Most other ships of that time smelled of garbage and damp cargo.

A model of the *Mayflower* sits in the waters off Massachusetts.

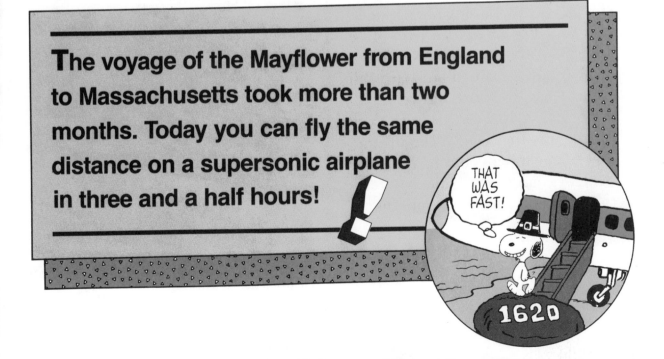

The voyage of the Mayflower from England to Massachusetts took more than two months. Today you can fly the same distance on a supersonic airplane in three and a half hours!

THAT WAS FAST!

1620

SCHOONERS, CLIPPER SHIPS, AND WINDJAMMERS

THREE-MASTED SCHOONER

What is a schooner?

A schooner is a large sailboat. It was popular as a fishing boat in New England in the 1700s. In those days, it had from two to seven masts. Although schooners aren't used much today, some still exist. Most of these have two or three masts and are used mostly for fun.

What were the fastest sailing ships?

Clipper ships were the fastest and the most beautiful sailing ships. Their beauty and speed came from the way they were built. They had long, sleek bodies and lots of sails. Some had as many as 35 sails.

Clipper ships were used during the mid-1800s. At that time, the United States and East Asia, especially China, were doing a great deal of trading. Clippers carried tea, coffee, and spices. These products would spoil if they remained on board ship for too long, so speed was very important. Clipper ships were named for the way they could "clip off the miles." A clipper could travel from the east coast of the United States to China and back in six months.

Clipper ships were the fastest sailing ships.

What were windjammers?

Windjammers were iron sailing ships with four masts. They became popular just after clipper ships. They, too, were used for trading and carrying cargo. Windjammers were huge and strong, perfect for sailing in bad weather and on rough seas.

Did any of these sailing ships carry passengers?

Almost all carried passengers as well as cargo. However, these ships sailed only when the weather was good, so passengers couldn't plan their trips ahead of time.

In the mid-1800s, packet ships became popular. They sailed at a set time, no matter what. The ship owners also made sure that first-class passengers were comfortable, so packet ships became very popular with rich ocean travelers.

RACING WITH THE WIND

What are racing sailboats made of?

Racing sailboats are very light and are made of wood, plastic, light metal, or fiberglass. They are fast and easy to handle. Modern sails are made of nylon or polyester, similar to the material of a windbreaker or winter jacket.

Are large sailboats ever used for racing?

Yes. For ocean racing, sailors must have a large boat. Because ocean races may be more than 1,300 miles long, the boats must be well built and able to handle rough waters. A boat called the 12-meter racer is the type most often used in the big race called the America's Cup. In 1988, however, the United States won the America's Cup with a type of sailboat called a catamaran.

What is a yacht?

The word *yacht* is used to describe sailing boats as small as a one-person, eight-foot dinghy to huge powerboats as long as 20 taxicabs in a row. Yachts can be used for pleasure cruising or full speed racing.

Dinghies and multihulls are two kinds of racing yachts. Each of these types of boats is built to guidelines for its particular group, or class. For each type of boat, there are many classes, based on length, sail size, and weight. Boat racers usually race against similar boats so that the race is a test of sailing skill, not of who has the biggest engine or largest sail.

These catamarans are locked in a close race!

What is a catamaran?

A catamaran is a sailboat with two separate hulls that are joined. A hull is the body, or frame, of a boat. In a catamaran, a little space is left between the hulls. "Cats," as these unusual-looking boats are called, are very fast. The two hulls cause less drag, making the cat a very fast boat.

Catamarans were invented by people who lived in the South Seas—a part of the Pacific Ocean. There, the natives used logs to make the two hulls. They used paddles and sometimes added sails to make their cats move. People still sail catamarans today.

CHAPTER 8

Rowing and sailing can be lots of fun, but how can you make a boat move without oars or a breeze? Over the years, inventors have come up with a few ways to power boats. If you want to see how, then hold on. We're ready to move, full steam ahead!

FULL STEAM AHEAD

EARLY STEAMBOATS AND THE PADDLE WHEEL

When did people start using steamboats?

The first workable steamboat was built in 1787 by an American named John Fitch. The boat had six long paddles on each side—like an overgrown canoe! The boat's paddles got their power from a steam engine.

Three years later, Fitch improved his model and put the paddles at the back. He then started taking passengers and cargo up and down the Delaware River. However, the engine was so large that there was very little room for the cargo, and not many people were interested in traveling on such a noisy boat. Fitch's steamboat service failed.

What was Fulton's Folly?

In 1807, Robert Fulton built the *Clermont*, the first successful steamboat. At first, people thought that building a steamboat was foolish. They referred to the boat as "Fulton's Folly," but Fulton combined the best features from other steamboats. Soon, the *Clermont* was making regular trips along New York's Hudson River.

HA HA HA HA!!

People laughed when Fulton first built the *Clermont*. After his steamboat became a success, Fulton had the last laugh!

Though the Clermont had room to seat 24 passengers, only 14 people were brave enough to go on its first trip. One month later, 90 passengers crowded on board!

What did the *Clermont* look like?

The *Clermont* was a long, thin boat. It had a smokestack that coughed out black smoke. Even though it had a steam engine, there were sails in case the engine broke down. It did not have canoe paddles like John Fitch's boat. Instead, the *Clermont* had a paddle wheel on each side.

A paddle-wheel boat churns through a river's water.

What is a paddle wheel?

A paddle wheel is a huge wheel with a series of flat paddles attached to it. Part of the wheel is always underwater. The power from a steam engine turns the wheel. As the paddles push the water, they move the boat forward.

Where were paddle-wheel boats used?

Paddle-wheel boats were used mostly on rivers. Sailboats move slowly on rivers because there isn't much wind there. Since paddle-wheel boats are powered by steam, not wind, they move quickly. Steamboats were popular on the Ohio and Mississippi rivers.

In 1986, a paddle-wheel boat was built from 40,000 milk cartons. The boat was named the Milky Wave and actually sailed with passengers!

What was a showboat?

A showboat was a paddle-wheel steamboat used as a traveling theater. In the 1800s, gaily decorated showboats brought plays, circuses, and live music to towns along the Mississippi River. Some boats even carried zoos and museums! Often, the show was held right on the boat. Other times, the showboat pulled a flat boat, called a barge, behind it. Then the theater was on the barge.

What was the first steamship to cross the Atlantic?

The paddle-wheel boat *Savannah* crossed the ocean in 1819. It left its home in Georgia and headed for Liverpool, England. Although many people believed that such a "steam coffin" would never make it all the way across the Atlantic Ocean, the *Savannah* made it to England—29 days later!

Twenty-nine days was not a record time for a ship to cross the Atlantic. Any packet ship of the day could have made the trip in that amount of time—or even less. Why wasn't the *Savannah's* trip faster? The reason is that the *Savannah* was built as a sailing ship. A steam engine and paddle wheels were added later. Most of the first Atlantic crossing was made using sail power. The *Savannah* had only enough fuel to run its engine for about 85 hours. The *Savannah's* trip was a first—but only a small beginning for steam.

When was the first all-steam ocean crossing?

The first all-steam crossing took place 19 years later, in 1838. The *Sirius* (SIR-ee-us) made the trip from Ireland to the east coast of the United States in 18½ days. By the 1840s, many steamships were making trips across the Atlantic Ocean.

Why don't we see paddle-wheel boats anymore?

The paddle wheel was replaced by the propeller. Starting in 1816, propellers were installed in some boats. Others still had paddle wheels. Great arguments took place as to which was better. In 1845, races were held between two nearly identical British ships, the *Rattler* and the *Alecto*. The *Rattler* had a propeller; the *Alecto* had a paddle wheel. The *Rattler* won every race! Soon after that, propellers replaced paddle wheels.

MODERN STEAMSHIPS

What do steamships look like today?

You have probably seen pictures of huge ocean liners such as the *Queen Elizabeth 2*. You may even have seen the actual liners. You can recognize them by their large smokestacks. Most ships with smokestacks are steamships, but some have diesel engines, and others use atomic energy.

Queen Elizabeth 2

How long does it take a steamship to cross the ocean today?

A fast steamship can cross the Atlantic Ocean between New York and Southampton, England, in 5½ days. It takes about 12 days for a steamship to cross the Pacific Ocean from Seattle, Washington, to Kobe, Japan.

What is it like to travel on a modern ocean liner?

A modern ocean liner is like a floating hotel. Once on board, it's easy to forget you're on a ship. The rooms are something like hotel rooms, and every modern convenience is right at your fingertips. There are restaurants, shops, game rooms, elevators, gymnasiums, swimming pools, and theaters.

NOW THIS IS THE LIFE!

CHAPTER 9

BOATS ON PARADE

From motor boats to cargo ships to ferries, boats have many different uses. Do you hear the whistle blowing? Three toots means Snoopy and the *Peanuts* gang are ready to shove off for a tour of boats, large and small.

THE ALL-PURPOSE MOTORBOAT

What is a motorboat?

A motorboat is the type of boat you see most often on lakes and rivers and in marinas—basins of water in which boats are docked. A motorboat is used for fun, fishing, transportation, rescue operations, police patrols, and even water-skiing. Motorboats come in many different sizes, just like sailboats. Motorboats have either an outboard motor or an inboard engine to make them move. An outboard motor is one attached to the outside of a boat. An inboard engine is one built right into the boat. The sailor uses a steering wheel to make turns.

BOATS FOR FUN

PEDAL FASTER, SCHROEDER, WE HAVE TO CATCH THAT SPEED BOAT!

What is a pedal boat?

A pedal boat is a cross between a bicycle and a boat. Pedal boats have no motors or sails or paddles. They have two seats and foot pedals. Pedal boats don't move quickly. They are usually made of plastic and are used only for fun.

The sleek design of this racing boat allows it to cut through the water at high speeds.

What is a cigarette boat?

Originally, "Cigarette" was the brand name of one of the first superfast powerboats. Today, it has come to mean any thin, fast sportboat. These boats usually measure between 20 and 45 feet in length. Cigarette boats are made of lightweight fiberglass and may be powered by three engines. Their needle-nose design cuts down drag, allowing some cigarette boats to reach speeds of 100 miles per hour.

What are some features of cruising yachts?

Cruising yachts trade speed for comfort and seaworthiness. All the comforts of home—from sleeping bunks to a kitchen—can be found on most larger cruising yachts. Today's yachts also have the most modern sailing instruments such as radar and long-range radio communication (up to 400 miles) to help navigate, or steer, the boat.

CARGO SHIPS

What is a cargo ship?

A cargo ship carries goods for trading. The old clipper ships were cargo ships, carrying tea and spices from China to the United States. They needed to be fast so that the cargo would not spoil before it could be unloaded. Today, many cargo ships have refrigerators on them.

Modern cargo ships are divided into four categories according to the things they carry. General cargo ships carry things that are put in packages, such as food, machinery, and clothing. Tankers carry oil or other liquids. Dry bulk carriers carry unpackaged goods such as coal or grain. Multipurpose ships can carry several different kinds of cargo at once.

Large electric cranes lift boxes and barrels onto and off of cargo ships. Once the cargo is aboard, crew members store it.

STAND ASIDE, SWABBIE... A CAPTAIN HAS IMPORTANT DUTIES TO ATTEND!

What is a supertanker?

A supertanker is a very large oil-carrying tanker. Except for some ships in the military, supertankers are the biggest ships. They are often longer than three football fields in a row! Supertankers are slower than other types of large ships, but they provide the cheapest way to carry oil. The liquid cargo that tanker ships carry is pumped on and off the tanker through special hoses.

A supertanker can travel only through large, deep bodies of water.

88

BARGES, TUGBOATS, FIREBOATS, AND FERRIES

What is a barge?

A barge is a flat-bottomed boat used to carry heavy freight, such as coal or steel. It usually has square ends that make docking and unloading easy.

In the old days, barges had no motors. They were pulled by horses or oxen. The animals would walk on the land next to the river or canal, pulling ropes attached to the barge. Now this towing work is usually done by tugboats. Some modern barges have their own motors. These barges can carry up to 20 million pounds of freight.

These tugboats are hard at work pulling an oil rig setup out to sea.

What are tugboats?

Tugboats are small, powerful boats. They are used to tow and guide bigger boats and ships into or out of a harbor. Tugs are used to pull large ocean liners and cargo ships through shallow waters or narrow areas. Without the tugs, large ships have a hard time moving through such small places. Some tugboats tow damaged ships into harbors.

Modern tugboats get their power from diesel engines. In the 1800s, tugs were driven by steam-powered paddle wheels.

What is a fireboat?

A fireboat puts out fires on ships and piers. It is like a fire engine on the water. Most big ports have at least one fireboat. Fireboats are equipped with powerful water guns that shoot great streams of water at the fire. A nozzle at the top of a tall tower shoots water the farthest. It can aim water at the deck or the inside of a burning ship. When big passenger liners come into a harbor, fireboats sometimes greet them by spraying water high into the air.

What is a ferry?

A ferry is a boat that carries people across a small body of water, such as a lake or a river. Some ferries carry people over larger bodies of water. However, all ferries travel back and forth between two ports on a regular schedule. Some ferry rides take five minutes. Others take two days. The ferries that make long trips have dining rooms and sleeping compartments.

This ferry runs between the state of Washington and its neighboring islands, the San Juan Islands.

Often, people bring bicycles on ferries. Larger ferries allow people to bring their cars, and some ferries are even large enough to carry railroad trains. Those ferries have their own tracks. That way, a whole train can ride right onto a train ferry and then ride off again. Most ferries are run by diesel or steam engines. In some places, however, ferries are pushed along with poles, or pulled by people or animals on a nearby shore or riverbank.

MILITARY SHIPS

What are today's military ships like?

From submarines that run silently deep under the water to ships that glide above it, today's military ships come in all shapes and sizes. The U.S. Navy's fleet includes 669 ships of war and 640 submarines. There are cruisers that launch guided missiles, aircraft carriers that can carry as many as 80 planes, and battleships that can use their guns to hit targets hundreds of miles away.

These warships use modern technology such as computers and advanced radar systems to spot their enemies. Many of them also use nuclear power, which allows them to go hundreds of thousands of miles without refueling.

What is "Old Ironsides"?

"Old Ironsides" is the nickname for a battleship called the *Constitution*. It had 44 guns and was one of the first warships of the United States. The *Constitution* won more battles than any other ship. It fought most of its famous battles during the War of 1812. Throughout all its fights, the hull was never damaged. That is why the ship was called "Old Ironsides."

Women were not allowed to work on the *Constitution* when it was a battleship. A woman named Lucy Brewer didn't like that. She dressed up in men's clothing and fooled the Marines!

WE LUCYS HAVE ALWAYS BEEN ABLE TO GET OUR WAY!

When did a plane first take off from a ship?

In 1910, an American pilot named Eugene Ely launched a plane from a boat. Using a ramp built on the navy cruiser U.S.S. *Birmingham*, Ely flew his plane two and a half miles from the ship to a soft ground landing.

From above, this aircraft carrier looks like a floating airport!

What is an aircraft carrier?

An aircraft carrier is a huge military ship that carries aircraft. Planes can take off from and land on its deck. This floating airport helps navies use planes to find and attack enemy ships. A carrier has a runway on top and a flight deck below for storing and repairing planes.

BOATS FROM FARAWAY PLACES

What are gondolas?

Gondolas are long, thin rowboats often used as water taxis. They are popular in Venice, Italy. Instead of roads, most of Venice has canals—narrow inland water-ways. People there use boats instead of cars.

At the back of a gon-dola stands the gon-dolier—the person who runs the boat. The gon-dolier uses a long pole to push the gondola.

A junk sits in the waters off Hong Kong.

What is a junk?

A junk is a kind of wooden sailboat. It was first used by the Chinese a few hundred years ago. If you go to the Orient today, you will still see many junks. They are usually painted in bright colors. White circles on the front stand for eyes. People who sail junks believe that these eyes are the boats' guiding spirits that watch for danger.

Junks have flat bot-toms and high sterns. The stern is the back of a boat. Junks have two or more four-cornered sails. Compared to mod-ern boats, junks are slow, so some people put motors on their junks.

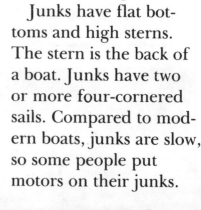

Hong Kong is famous for its crowded sampan city.

What is a sampan?

A sampan is a small, fast-moving boat found chiefly in China, Japan, and other countries in the Orient. They are also used in India and on many islands in the Pacific Ocean.

A sampan is usually flat-bottomed. Often this type of boat is used as a house for a family. Some sampans are also used for carrying freight or products to be sold at market. Not all sampans look alike, but most have an arched or boxed cabin covered with straw mats. A cabin is the place on the boat where people live.

Most sampans are equipped with both oars and sails. If there's no wind for sailing, the owners can always row the boat.

Where is there a floating sampan "city"?

In Hong Kong, a city on the south coast of China, groups of people live and work on sampans docked right next to each other. Some sampans are homes. Others are food stores and restaurants. Many of the sampans are very old. Their cabin covers are full of patches.

93

Some boats don't exactly float. They skim over the water or glide on ice or travel beneath the sea. Let's hop on board with the *Peanuts* gang for some oceangoing fun!

IS THAT REALLY A BOAT?

BOATS ABOVE THE WATER

What is a hydrofoil?

A hydrofoil is a boat that skims very quickly over the water. Its hull stays just above the surface. Only the hydrofoil's "sea wings" stay in the water. These work very much like airplane wings. When a plane picks up speed, the wings lift it into the air. In the same way, when the hydrofoil picks up speed, its sea wings lift it out of the water. There is less drag from the water, so the hydrofoil can travel much faster than other kinds of boats. Hydrofoils are used for passenger travel and by the military.

This hydrofoil can move faster because of the red "sea wings" beneath its hull.

A hovercraft whizzes over the surface of the water!

What is a hovercraft?

A hovercraft is also called an air-cushioned vehicle (ACV). It can be driven on water or land. It has fans or propellers that take in air at the top and blow it out the bottom. A hovercraft is lifted above the surface of the water by the air that comes out under it. These amazing vehicles shouldn't really be called boats, since they travel above the surface of the water, not in it. A hovercraft can go almost anywhere—swamps, mud, river rapids, even over ice.

A sailor keeps his iceboat balanced as it speeds across the ice.

What is an iceboat?

An iceboat is a narrow, pointed sailboat that travels on ice instead of on water. It can do this because it rests on runners—usually three. They look something like short skis. An iceboat's sails are usually very large. They catch the wind and make the iceboat move, just as they would any sailboat.

Iceboating (also called ice yachting) has long been a favorite pastime in Norway, Sweden, Denmark, and Finland. There, the water is frozen much of the year. Today, iceboating is a popular winter sport in many other countries, as well.

What is an icebreaker?

An icebreaker is a special kind of ship designed to break through ice. Its bow is covered with strong metal that acts as armor. An icebreaker has propellers both in back and in front. This makes the ship easier to handle. To break the ice, the ship's bow climbs partly up onto the ice. The weight of the ship causes the ice to break. In order to push the heavy ship onto the ice, the icebreaker's engines must be very powerful.

SUBMARINES

Are any other boats good for traveling in icy places?

Yes. Submarines—called subs for short—can travel where ice usually stops most ships. Submarines go underneath the ice. By traveling under it, a nuclear submarine named the *Nautilus* reached the North Pole in 1958. The next year, a nuclear sub named the *Skate* broke through the North Pole ice.

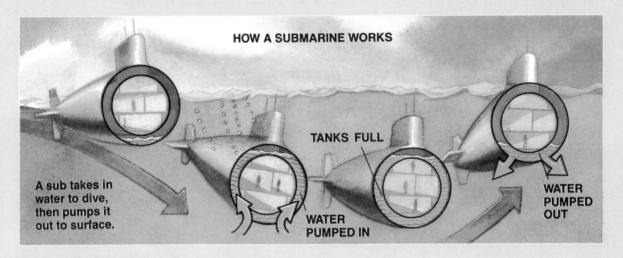

HOW A SUBMARINE WORKS

A sub takes in water to dive, then pumps it out to surface.

WATER PUMPED IN

TANKS FULL

WATER PUMPED OUT

How else are submarines used?

Oceanographers (o-shun-OG-ruh-furz) are scientists who study ocean life. They use submarines to explore the bottom of the sea, and to help them get valuable minerals from the ocean floor. Small submarines, called submersibles, are used to explore sunken ships.

How does a submarine go up and down?

In order to dive, or go down, a submarine takes water into special storage tanks. The water adds weight to a submarine. When the sub gets heavy enough, it sinks. To surface, or go up, air is forced into the tanks, and the water is blown out. The submarine now rises to the surface of the sea. It will stay on the surface until the tanks are filled with water again.

Once underwater, a sub can move up or down by using steel fins at the rear of the ship. These are called diving planes. When the fins are tilted down, the submarine will dive. When they are tilted up, the sub will rise.

What were the first subs like?

Early submarine experiments date back hundreds of years. In the 1620s, a Dutch engineer named Cornelius Drebbel built the first submarine. It was a leather-covered rowing boat that could travel underwater. Twelve men with oars sat inside and rowed. The inventor used a chemical to keep the air breathable, but he kept the formula a secret, so no one knows what the chemical was.

The first sub ever used in a war was called the *Turtle*. It was used in 1776 during the American Revolution. It attacked a British warship, but the attack was not successful. The British ship did not sink. The *Turtle* was shaped something like a turtle's shell. A man sat inside and turned a pole called a crankshaft. The crankshaft was attached to propellers. When the crankshaft moved, the propellers moved. Then the sub moved.

Where did breathable air come from in later submarines?

In the early 1900s, submarines could stay underwater only for short periods of time. The subs did not have any way to replace air. The problem was solved with a snorkel. This was a tube that came out of the top of the sub. It allowed fresh air to come into the cabin. With snorkels, subs could travel for long periods just below the surface of the water. They could not stay in deep water, however, for more than a few hours at a time.

Today, subs make their own oxygen from seawater, so they can stay underwater for a long time.

What kind of power do submarines use today?

Modern submarines use nuclear energy. It is the most powerful force known. Uranium (you-RAY-nee-um) is the fuel used for nuclear energy. One ounce of it gives out as much energy as is created by burning 100 tons of coal, so nuclear-powered subs can travel long distances without refueling.

I HATE IT WHEN WOODSTOCK PLAYS SUBMARINE IN MY WATER DISH!

Are any ships besides submarines powered by nuclear energy?

As we learned, nuclear energy has been used in a few, mostly military, U.S. and Soviet ships. Nuclear power for civilian ships is still in the experimental stage. The equipment needed is very bulky, and it's also very expensive. That's why most ships today are powered by diesel or steam engines.

A submarine moves slowly through ocean waters.

THE DIVING BELL

What's the deepest anyone has ever gone in the ocean?

Nearly 36,000 feet is the deepest. Since the sixteenth century, scientists have used diving bells—round, airtight containers—to go underwater. In 1960, two men went down 35,817 feet into the Pacific Ocean. They reached the deepest known part of the ocean. The long trip down took more than five hours and was made in a diving bell called a bathyscaphe (BATH-ih-skaff). A bathyscaphe carries heavy steel to make it sink. When the steel is dropped, the bathyscaphe gets lighter and comes up. Early diving bells were lowered into the water on heavy ropes or steel cables. Bathyscaphes carry oxygen in bottles, and chemicals for cleaning used air.

99

CHAPTER 11

ANCHORS AWEIGH!

An ocean is a very big place indeed. It stretches as far as the eye can see and seems like an easy place in which to get lost. Well, let's join Captain Charlie Brown and his mates to see how ships set sail and come back again, safe and sound, and without getting lost.

THE CAPTAIN'S LOG

Why does a ship's captain keep a log book?

A ship's log is the daily record of a trip. The ship's captain is usually the one who keeps the log. The captain writes down all the important details of the trip. These include the exact route, events that happen on board, and radio messages. Over the years, ships' log books have been a great help in piecing together facts about the history of sea travel. A log is also important if a ship has an accident. It helps uncover the reason for the mishap.

MAPS, COMPASSES, RADAR, AND SOUND WAVES

Does a ship's captain have a road map to follow?

Yes, in a way. A ship's captain has the help of one or more specially trained people called navigators. Before beginning a voyage, the navigators mark the ship's route on a special sea map, called a chart. During the trip, they keep track of the ship's position by using radar and other electronic equipment. The captain uses this information to stay on the course marked on the chart.

In ancient times, sailors figured out their direction by looking at the stars. By the 1100s, sailors were using compasses to tell direction.

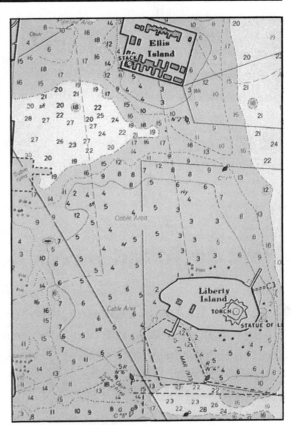

Charts such as this one help navigators mark a ship's route.

How does a compass work?

A compass needle is a magnet. The Earth's North and South poles also are magnets. If a compass needle is free to turn, it lines itself up with the Earth's magnetic poles. One end points toward the north. The other end points toward the south.

Letters painted on a dial under the needle show all the directions. A sailor just has to look at the compass to see which way the ship is going. For example, if the north end of the compass needle points toward the back of the ship, that means north is behind it. The ship is traveling south.

How does radar help ships?

The word *radar* stands for **ra**dio **d**etecting **a**nd **r**anging. It is a way of telling direction and distance by using radio waves. A radar antenna sends out special signals called radio waves. When these waves bump into a solid object, they bounce back to the antenna. The radar device measures the time it takes for the waves to travel back and forth. Then it figures out where the object is.

Radar will warn a ship's captain—even in fog—of something in the way of the ship.

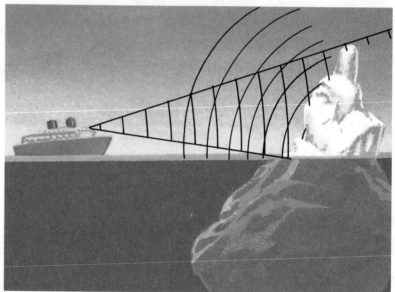

Radio waves sent by a ship's radar bump into an iceberg and bounce back to the ship's antenna. Now the ship won't run into the iceberg!

How do sound waves help ships?

Sailors can't see the floor of the ocean, so they use sound to help them get a picture of it. An instrument called a depth sounder sends a high-pitched sound that travels to the ocean bottom. From there, its echo bounces back to the surface. The depth sounder measures how long it takes for the echo to bounce back. If it takes a long time, it means that the echo had to bounce back a long distance and that the water is deep. This process is called *sonar*, which stands for **so**und **na**vigation **r**anging. Some depth sounders not only tell the depth of the water, they also use echoes to detect fish!

DOCKING THE BOAT

What is an anchor?

An anchor is a heavy metal object attached to the boat by a long rope or chain. When the anchor is thrown overboard, its pointed hook digs into the bottom of the ocean, river, or lake. It keeps the boat from drifting away. Before leaving a boat, a good sailor pulls on the anchor to make sure it has a firm hold in the ground. Boats need anchors unless they are tied to a dock.

The famous oceanographer Jacques Cousteau (ZHOCK koo-STOE) dropped an anchor 24,600 feet into the Atlantic Ocean!

How are boats docked?

A small boat is easy to dock. The skipper, or captain, just slows the boat down and heads for the dock at an angle. Because the boat is moving so slowly, it rubs up next to the dock very gently. Sometimes bumpers on the dock or boat give extra protection. Once the boat is docked, the skipper jumps off and ties it up.

A big ship is harder to dock. While a harbor pilot steers the ship, a tugboat pushes it into place. Many people are needed to help tie up the ship.

What is a harbor pilot?

When a ship comes into or leaves a harbor, a harbor pilot must be on board. His job is to guide the ship through the harbor. The pilot is familiar with the tides, the winds, and all the specially shaped or marked floats in the water. Such floating markers are called buoys (BOO-ees).

What is the difference between a port and a harbor?

Sometimes people use the words *port* and *harbor* to mean the same thing, but there is a difference. All ports are harbors, but not all harbors are ports.

A harbor is a part of the body of water that is deep enough for anchoring boats or ships. A harbor is partly surrounded by land, or else it has piers that extend into the water. The land or the piers protect boats from strong winds and currents and rough water. A port is a special kind of harbor. Passengers and freight can be loaded or unloaded there. A large, busy port usually has cranes for handling heavy freight, warehouses for storing things, radio equipment, repair services, fueling stations, and even restaurants.

What are buoys used for?

Buoys help sailors find their way in strange waters. Most buoys are used as channel markers. A channel is the bottom of a body of water. Channel markers warn sailors of shallow or rocky areas in the water or give other important information. Some buoys are used to anchor boats.

AHOY!

104

DRY DOCK

This large ship is in dry dock to be repaired.

What are dry docks?

In order for a ship to be repaired and painted, it must be taken out of the water. Since large ships are heavy, special docks called dry docks were invented. There are two main kinds, the floating dock and the graving dock.

What is a floating dock?

A floating dry dock is a floating platform with walls on two sides. Water is pumped into it. The dock sinks, and the ship moves onto it. When the water is pumped out again, the dock rises once more to the surface. Now the ship is in dry dock and ready for repair.

What is a graving dock?

A graving dry dock is a deep concrete tub sunk into the ground. One end of it opens into the harbor. When the ship enters, a gate closes the tub off from the harbor. Then, as the water is pumped out, the ship sinks to the bottom of the tub. When all the water is out, the ship is in dry dock.

The Unsinkable *Titanic*

The *Titanic* was the largest ocean liner in the world when it was built. Experts said that the ship would never sink, but on its very first trip, the *Titanic* hit an iceberg and sank. The lifeboats could hold only half of the people on the ship, so many people drowned. The wreck is still at the bottom of the ocean.

Using a submersible—an underwater vehicle— called *Alvin*, scientists recently discovered the wreck. *Alvin* was able to dive 13,000 feet, much deeper than other submersibles had gone. With the help of a camera, the rest of the world was able to see photographs of the *Titanic's* ballroom, complete with chandelier, railing, and a bottle of champagne!

ALVIN, COME BACK!

Jet Set

It's a scooter! It's a water jet! No, it's just a super jet ski, a cross between a motorcycle and water skis. An engine draws water in from under the jet ski, then blows it out the back. This stream pushes the jet ski through the water very quickly. The jet ski has a platform on the back where the rider can lie down, kneel, or stand.

This is one vehicle you'll never lose. If you fall off, the jet ski turns slowly in a circle, giving you a chance to catch your breath and swim back to it.

A jet skier guides her jet ski into a turn.

IF YOU'RE HUNGRY AND YOU REALLY WANT YOUR SUPPER, YOU HAVE TO KNOW HOW TO STARE AT THE BACK DOOR...

YOUR EYES HAVE TO FLASH LIKE THE BEACON FROM A LIGHTHOUSE!

A GOOD STARE CAN PEEL THE PAINT RIGHT OFF THE DOOR!

Night Lights

The lights and signals from lighthouses help sailors steer their ships in the right direction. Lightships are floating lighthouses that are permanently anchored near the shore. Their powerful lights and foghorns warn sailors of nearby hazards such as rocks or shallow water.

Computer Sailing

A French sailing ship called the *Wind Song* uses a computer to control its sails. There are four masts on this large sailboat. At 440 feet long, it is the longest sailboat used today.

Getting to the Bottom

Ships called dredges have special digging tools. They bring up mud and gravel from the bottom of oceans, rivers, or lakes. Dredges are used to make shipping channels deeper and wider so large vessels can get through. They are also used to dig for valuable minerals or to build up land along the shore.

Tied in Knots?

Instead of giving speed in "miles per hour," sailors refer to "knots." A knot equals 1.15 miles per hour. To change from miles per hour to knots, divide by 1.15. For example, 38 miles per hour is the same speed as 33 knots.

MY BRAIN GETS TIED IN KNOTS JUST TRYING TO UNDERSTAND THAT!

Long ago, people tried all sorts of ways to fly like the birds. It wasn't until hot-air balloons were invented, though, that people finally got off the ground safely. Let's climb aboard Linus's balloon and travel back through time to see how people first began to reach for the sky.

UP, UP, AND AWAY

CHAPTER 12

GETTING OFF THE GROUND

How did people first try to fly?

People made wings of feathers and tried to fly like birds. They attached their homemade wings to their arms and jumped from high places. Usually, they were killed or badly injured.

In 1490, an Italian named Danti made some wings to help him fly. For a moment, it looked as if they would work, but Danti crashed to the ground.

In about 1500, a man named Wan Ho tried to fly in China. He tied 47 rockets to the back of his chair. Then he strapped himself in. His friends attached two kites to his chair, then lit the rockets. There was a big explosion. Wan Ho was never seen again.

© 1971 Ripley Entertainment, Inc.
Registered Trademark of
Ripley Entertainment, Inc.

IN 1742 THE MARQUIS de BACQUEVILLE BROKE BOTH OF HIS LEGS TRYING TO FLY ACROSS THE SEINE RIVER in France WITH GIANT WINGS TIED TO HIS HANDS AND FEET!

BALLOONS

What was the first successful flying machine?

The first successful flying machine was a balloon built by Joseph and Jacques Montgolfier (ZHOCK mawn-gawl-FYAY) in 1782. One day, while watching a fire in their fireplace, the brothers noticed that the smoke went up the chimney. The brothers wondered why. When Joseph and Jacques trapped some smoke in a paper bag, the bag floated in the air.

Later that year, they took a bag that measured 35 feet around and weighed 300 pounds. The brothers made a smoky fire and floated the bag over the fire. It rose more than a mile high before it cooled off and came back down. This was the first balloon flight. Later, people discovered that it was hot air and not smoke that made balloons rise.

A propane heater is used to heat air to inflate this balloon.

BALLOON RISES

BALLOON DESCENDS

When air is heated, cold air is forced out.

When burner is turned off, cool air rushes in.

Burner

Basket

How does the hot-air balloon work?

A hot-air balloon is a large, airtight cloth or plastic bag that is open at the bottom. The balloon is filled with heated air. Hot air is lighter than cool air, so hot air rises. The hot air inside the balloon is lighter than the cool air outside, so the balloon rises. When the heated air cools and becomes as heavy as the air outside, the balloon will stop rising and come down.

A hot-air balloon carries people in a basket attached to its bottom end. Hot-air balloons also carry propane heaters to heat air. A blast from the heater causes the balloon to rise higher. When the passengers want to come down, they can open the top of the balloon to let out heated air.

111

Who was the first person to fly?

Pilatre de Rozier (pee-LAH-truh DUH row-ZYAY) of France was the first person to fly. A duck, a sheep, and a rooster had already flown in a Montgolfier balloon. Now it was a person's turn. King Louis XVI (the six-teenth) offered to send up a prisoner who was to be executed soon, but de Rozier begged to go.

On October 15, 1783, de Rozier climbed aboard the balloon. It rose 80 feet into the air, about as high as a six-story building. It proba-bly would have gone higher, but it was held down by a rope. Man's first flight lasted four and a half minutes.

Early balloons carried sponges and a bucket of water for putting out the fires that kept starting!

YOU FLY IN A BALLOON? YOU CAN'T EVEN FLY A KITE, BIG BROTHER!

In 1870, a man named Leon Gambetta used a hot-air balloon to escape from Paris, France, when Germany was attacking the city.

How did people first use balloons?

After de Rozier's first balloon flight, people tried to see how far they could go in balloons. A Frenchman, Jean Pierre Blanchard (ZHON PYAIR blon-SHAR), crossed the English Channel in a balloon in 1785. A balloon called the *Great Balloon of Nassau* sailed 500 miles, from London, England, to Germany in 1836. Balloons were also used in World War I and other wars to observe enemy armies.

How fast can a balloon go?

A balloon has no moving power of its own. It can travel only as fast as the wind that carries it.

POOF! POOF! POOF!

Why did people stop using balloons for travel?

Balloon flight can't be controlled. Some people tried to steer balloons by using sails. Others tried oars. A few people tried paddles. Nothing worked. When better airships were invented, people lost interest in balloons.

How are balloons used today?

Scientists use very big plastic balloons to gather weather information. These balloons carry equipment to record temperature, humidity (moisture), air pressure, and wind speeds. This information is sent back to the scientists by radio equipment, which is also carried by the balloons.

If a weather balloon breaks, the instruments it carries float back to the Earth in a bright red parachute.

How else are balloons used?

Today, people travel in balloons as a sport. Balloon races were held in the United States as early as 1906, and today, balloonists still participate in races and contests for fun. Many races, such as the Albuquerque Balloon Fiesta in New Mexico, aren't really competitive races. They are more like festivals, where people gather to enjoy watching or riding in the brightly-colored balloons. Races or festivals are usually held in a place where there is a lot of wide, open space. Sometimes as many as 500 balloons lift off in succession!

No, it's not a plane. It's a balloon built to resemble one!

What do today's balloons look like?

Today's balloons come in many different shapes. Some are still round, like the first balloon built by the Montgolfier brothers. Others, like some you might see at a balloon festival, resemble cartoon characters or everyday objects. There are balloons shaped like Donald Duck's head, a hamburger, and even a cow jumping over a moon!

DIRIGIBLES

What first replaced the balloon?

The dirigible (DIR-ih-juh-bull), also called an airship, first replaced the balloon. Like a balloon, a dirigible is wingless and weighs less than air. Unlike a balloon, it has a propeller and an engine and can be steered with a rudder. The rudder is a movable part at the rear of a dirigible. When the pilot moves the rudder to the right, the front of the airship moves right. When the rudder is moved left, the front of the airship moves left.

A rubberlike skin fits over a rigid frame in most dirigibles. The skin is filled with gas that weighs less than air. The gas inside the dirigible gives the airship its shape. A dirigible usually looks like a giant cigar. The first successful dirigible was flown in 1852. It had a top speed of six miles an hour. That's about as fast as a brisk roller-skate ride.

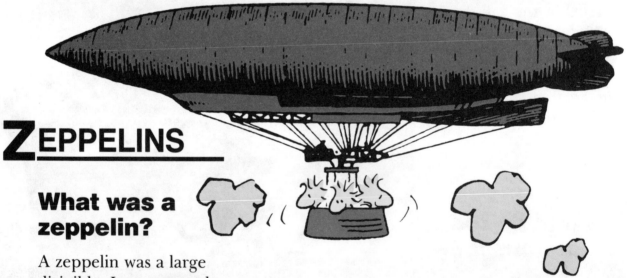

ZEPPELINS

What was a zeppelin?

A zeppelin was a large dirigible. It was named for the man who designed it, Count Ferdinand von Zeppelin of Germany.

The first zeppelin was built in 1900. It had a cigar-shaped aluminum frame and weighed 25,350 pounds, about as much as three elephants.

How were zeppelins used?

Zeppelins carried passengers who wanted to go sightseeing. Regularly scheduled zeppelin flights were made across the Atlantic Ocean. Count von Zeppelin began an airship company that carried 34,288 people in four years without an accident. During World War I, zeppelins had another use. The Germans built 100 zeppelins for military use. Their mission: bombing London!

In 1928, ten years after World War I, the Graf Zeppelin, a large German zeppelin, flew around the world in 22 days!

What was the *Hindenburg*?

The *Hindenburg* was the largest airship ever built. It was a zeppelin 803 feet long. That's about as long as 54 cars in a line. The *Hindenburg* was 135 feet wide—about as wide as 9 cars in a line. The *Hindenburg* had a lounge, a piano, and paneled bedrooms. It made 35 trips across the Atlantic Ocean. On May 6, 1937, it suddenly exploded and burned as it was trying to land at Lakehurst, New Jersey. There were 97 people aboard. Thirty-six of them died. No one ever found out what caused the disaster, but zeppelins were filled with hydrogen gas, which people knew was very explosive. After the *Hindenburg* tragedy, hydrogen was never used in airships again, and zeppelins were never again manufactured.

The *Hindenburg* exploded on May 6, 1937.

Will zeppelins ever be used again?

Perhaps zeppelins will be used again in the future. Scientists today are beginning to think about lighter-than-air aircraft once again. A zeppelin, if powered by the most powerful energy in the world—atomic energy—might work well. Because atomic energy uses very little fuel, an atomic zeppelin would not have to be refueled very often. It could remain in the air for a week at a time. A zeppelin can stay still in the sky, so it could remain in one place while scientists studied the land and water below. The U.S. military wants to use zeppelins to patrol borders. Some people are sure that zeppelins will make a comeback.

BLIMPS

Snoopy is everywhere— even on a blimp!

© 1989 Metropolitan Life Insurance Company, NY, NY

I ATE THE WHOLE BAG, AND NOW I FEEL LIKE A BLIMP!

Are blimps the same as zeppelins?

Blimps are small dirigibles. They are usually filled with helium gas. No one is sure how the blimp got its nickname. The first model was called an A-limp. The B-limp was the improved version. Some say that B-limp was shortened to blimp. Others say the name came from the sound of a thumb thumping the blimp during the preflight check. If it sounded like "blimp," the inflation was correct. The few blimps around today are used for advertising.

118

Famous pilots have often become heroes around the world. Their sense of adventure and daredevil stunts have thrilled people in all corners of the Earth. What's that in the sky? Why, it's Woodstock, asking you to come along and meet some famous firsts in flight!

FAMOUS FLIERS

THE WRIGHT BROTHERS

Orville and Wilbur Wright

Who invented the airplane?

The Wright brothers invented the first safe, successful airplane. However, their first flight, near Kitty Hawk, North Carolina, didn't make great news. Nothing appeared in the newspapers on that day—December 17, 1903. A few days later, short items began to appear in newspapers across the country, but no one seemed very interested or impressed. Today, that flight is known around the world.

How long did the first airplane flight last?

Orville Wright took the *Flyer I* up in the air and flew it for 12 seconds. That same day, Wilbur Wright took turns with his brother flying their airplane. The next two flights lasted twice as long as the first one. On the fourth flight that day, the airplane stayed in the air for 59 seconds.

The pilot of Flyer I had to lie down to fly the plane. He balanced it by moving his hips!

What did the *Flyer I* look like?

The *Flyer I* was a biplane. That means it had two sets of wings, one above the other. The two propellers were behind the pilot. This kind of biplane was later called a pusher plane because the air flowed out the back, pushing the plane forward. In World War I, the propeller was moved to the front so that it "pulled" the plane.

Another Wright flyer—this one built by the brothers in 1908 at the request of the U.S. government.

The propellers on Flyer I were attached to the engine by a bicycle chain!

Flyer I

WITH A NAME LIKE WRIGHT, WHAT COULD BE WRONG?

121

FAMOUS FIRSTS

Who was the first person to fly across the sea?

Louis Blériot (loo-EE blay-RYO) flew across the English Channel from France to England in 1909. He showed that people from different countries could now visit each other fairly easily. Blériot received a reward for

Louis Blériot sits in the monoplane he flew across the English Channel.

his feat. When he completed the Channel crossing in his *Blériot XI* (eleven) monoplane, he won a prize of $5,000 from a British newspaper.

The Baroness de la Roche was the first woman pilot.

Who was the first woman pilot?

The Baroness de la Roche (DUH LAH RAWSH) was the first woman pilot. She made her first flight in 1908 without a pilot's license! Two years later, she was given one.

Who was the first person to cross the Atlantic Ocean?

The first crossing of the Atlantic Ocean was made in 1919 by a man named Albert C. Read. Four U.S. Navy seaplanes—NC-1, NC-2, NC-3, and NC-4—planned to make the journey. NC-4, Lieutenant Commander Read's plane, was the only one to make it. He and a five-man crew flew from Newfoundland in Canada to the Azores, which are islands in the middle of the Atlantic Ocean, and then on to Lisbon, Portugal.

When was the first nonstop flight made across the Atlantic?

Eighteen days later, two Englishmen named John Alcock and Arthur Brown flew nonstop from Newfoundland to Ireland. Their plane was a World War I military plane.

Wiley Post (left) and Harold Gatty (right) wave to cheering fans in New York City after completing the fastest trip around the world in 1931.

Who were the first men to circle around the world in a plane?

The U.S. Army Air Service sent out four planes in 1924. Two of them made it around the world. The pilots' names were Lowell Smith and Erik Nelson. The trip took 150 days.

Was 150 days the fastest trip at that time?

It wasn't even close to being the fastest. Zeppelins had made the trip around the world many years before planes did. The *Graf Zeppelin* made the trip in 21 days. Still, most airplane pilots knew they could break that record. In fact, in 1931, a pilot named Wiley Post and a navigator named Harold Gatty said they could do it in 10 days. Instead, they did it in 8 days, 15 hours, and 51 minutes.

FAMOUS FIRSTS

Who was the first person to fly solo, or alone, around the world?

Wiley Post did it again. Because Wiley did not have much education, people believed that he couldn't have made his first trip without Harold Gatty. This upset Wiley. He claimed he could make the trip by himself, and do it in 7 days. He did. He went around the world in 7 days, 18 hours, and 49 minutes.

123

LUCKY LINDY

Who was Lucky Lindy?

Lucky Lindy was the nickname of a man named Charles Lindbergh, one of the most famous fliers of all time. Even though he was the 79th person to cross the Atlantic, he was the first person to do it alone. Raymond Orteig, a New York City hotel owner, offered to give $25,000 to the first person to fly nonstop from New York to Paris. Charles Lindbergh accepted the challenge.

St. Louis businessmen paid for a plane, the *Spirit of St. Louis*, built specially for Lindbergh. Its cockpit was just the right size for his body, and it had five fuel tanks. To save space for fuel, Lindbergh didn't take even a parachute or radio.

When was Lindbergh's famous flight?

On May 20, 1927, Lindbergh took off early in the morning from Roosevelt Field in Garden City, New York. He flew his plane through fog, rain, and sleet. He hadn't slept the night before because he was so nervous, so he had to fight to stay awake on the long trip. He landed in Paris 33 hours and 30 minutes later. He had flown 3,600 miles.

Lindbergh brought along five sandwiches. Because he thought that food might put him to sleep, he ate only one and a half during the long trip!

How did Lindbergh start flying?

From almost the first time he saw a plane, Lindbergh knew that he wanted to fly. He started working as a stunt person with a barnstormer. He saved his money to buy a plane, then taught himself how to fly. For a while he worked as an airmail pilot.

What was barnstorming?

Barnstorming was a type of show that stunt pilots gave in the early days of airplanes. Barnstorming pilots flew their planes from one small town to another, stopping wherever a fair or festival was going on. Airplanes were an unusual sight then, so people gathered to watch. The pilot would swoop low over towns and nearby farms, and a stunt person accompanying the pilot would perform daring feats such as parachute jumps and walking on the plane's wings. When the plane landed, the pilot would sell short rides in it for about $5.

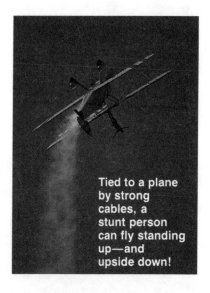

Tied to a plane by strong cables, a stunt person can fly standing up—and upside down!

What happened to the *Spirit of St. Louis*?

After Lindbergh made his famous flight to Paris, he and his plane were brought back on a Navy ship. Lindbergh now was a hero. After a tour of all 48 states, he gave his plane to a museum in Washington, D.C. You can still see the *Spirit of St. Louis* and many other famous planes at the Smithsonian National Air and Space Museum in Washington, D.C.

AMELIA EARHART

Who was Amelia Earhart?

Amelia Earhart was a famous pilot who achieved a lot of firsts. She was the first woman to receive the Distinguished Flying Cross award, and she was the first to fly alone across the United States in both directions. She was the first woman to cross the Atlantic as a passenger, and she was also the first woman (and second person) to cross it solo. Even though she made it across, she was forced to cut her flight short. When she was over Ireland, she noticed that her fuel tank was leaking. This forced her to land, but she did make it!

To prepare for her first long solo flight, Amelia Earhart practiced going without sleep or food for many days at a time. She didn't need all the practice. Her trip lasted only about 14 hours!

What finally happened to Amelia Earhart?

In 1937, she and her navigator, Fred Noonan, tried to fly a twin-engine airplane around the world. They didn't make it. A ship picked up a radio signal from their airplane. The plane was short of fuel over the Pacific Ocean. That was the last anyone heard from them. Planes and ships searched, but no trace of Amelia Earhart, Fred Noonan, or their plane was ever found.

CHAPTER 14

You hear the engines whirring. You see the silver jets soaring across the sky. How do those giant planes fly through the air? Fasten your seat belt, and Charlie Brown will take you on a trip through the clouds to show you all about flying.

FASTEN YOUR SEAT BELT

TAKING OFF

A big airplane has to gather a lot of speed before the lift force is strong enough to raise it off the ground.

How can a heavy plane stay up in the air?

When a plane is flying, it is being pulled up and down and backward and forward all at the same time. The force of gravity pulls the plane downward. Lift—the force made by the wings as they cut through the air—pushes it upward. The force of drag pulls the plane backward, while a force called thrust pushes it forward. Jet engines or propellers give thrust. A heavy plane in steady flight stays in the air for two reasons. The thrust from its engines or propellers equals the drag force, and the lift made by its wings equals the force of gravity on the plane (its weight).

What are runways used for?

An airplane needs a runway to take off and to land. An airplane must race across the ground to gather speed before the lift force is strong enough to raise it off the ground.

Small planes can leave the ground at speeds of only 30 to 40 miles an hour. That is slower than cars normally travel on a highway. Heavier planes may have to reach 100 miles an hour before they can lift into the air. That is almost twice the speed limit for cars on a highway.

Are runways used for anything else?

Runways are also used for landings. In a car, a driver has to start braking a good distance before actually stopping. The faster the car is going, the longer the distance has to be. If a driver brakes quickly, the car will jerk and everyone will be thrown forward. The same is true of planes. Pilots need long runways so that they can brake slowly and give the passengers a comfortable stop.

PARTS OF AN AIRPLANE

What are the most important parts of an airplane?

Modern airplanes have three main parts. They are the wings, the tail assembly, and the body. The body is called the fuselage (FYOO-suh-lahj).

How are the wings important?

The airplane's wings provide lift to push the plane into the sky. As long as the engines are providing thrust and speed at the same time, the airplane can stay up.

What is the tail assembly?

The tail assembly keeps the plane steady. It is made up of three parts: the rudder, the fin, and the stabilizer. The pilot swings the rudder to the right to move the plane right or to the left to move the plane left. The fin is the part of the tail assembly that keeps the plane steady in forward flight. The stabilizer keeps the airplane from wobbling up and down. Other tail parts called elevators are connected to the stabilizer. They help the plane go up and down during takeoffs and landings.

Why is the fuselage important?

This is where the passengers sit or where freight is stored. The fuselage also includes the cockpit, the place where the pilot sits. All the plane's controls are in the cockpit.

What are ailerons?

Ailerons (AY-luh-ronz) are movable flaps on the wings that let the pilot tilt the plane left or right. This is called banking. By banking the plane, the pilot makes it turn one way or the other. Other wing flaps give the plane stronger lift at the slower speeds of takeoff and landing.

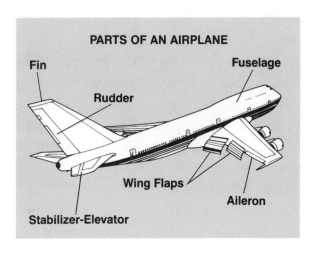

PARTS OF AN AIRPLANE

Fin

Rudder

Fuselage

Wing Flaps

Aileron

Stabilizer-Elevator

129

BECOMING A PILOT

How can you become a pilot?

Every pilot must have a license in order to fly an airplane. A person must be at least 16 years old to get a student's license, and 17 years old to get a regular license. Flying lessons are necessary, and they are expensive, too. Some people get their pilot's license by joining the armed forces, which has pilot training programs. Many colleges offer flight training programs. There are many things to learn about flying. Students usually take courses in weather, air science, and the rules of flying. A student pilot must spend at least 40 hours flying, first with a licensed instructor and then alone. The student must complete one 300-mile flight without having the instructor in the plane. Then the student takes a flight test, or check ride, with a licensed examiner on board. A pilot must also pass a written test and a physical examination by a doctor.

Every part of the plane must be checked before takeoff.

FLYING A PLANE

What happens to a plane before it is ready to take off?

An airplane is thoroughly checked by the airplane's safety crew before it is allowed to leave the airport. A person from the Federal Aviation Administration spotchecks the plane to be sure it is safe. Everything in the airplane must be working correctly. Mechanics who work on it are well trained. They know how to take an engine completely apart. They can put it together again so that it runs perfectly. A safety person checks the weight of the baggage, the passengers, and the cargo. The dispatcher decides the route the pilot will take and how high he or she should fly. The weather station tells the pilot what the weather conditions will be like during the flight.

The pilot and the flight crew check the instruments on the control panel. They use a checklist. The pilot names an instrument, and the copilot or flight engineer checks the instrument to be sure it is working right.

What happens when the plane is all set to go?

The pilot starts the engines. He or she speaks to the control tower by radio. The control tower tells the pilot which runway to use. The pilot taxis to the runway. Once the control tower gives clearance, the plane rolls down the runway. Then the pilot raises the nose and steers the plane into lift-off.

How can a plane fly upside down?

A plane can fly upside down because the same forces—lift, drag, thrust, and gravity—that pull on a right-side-up plane also pull on an upside-down plane. The only force that may not be strong in an upside-down plane is lift—the force made by the wings as they cut through the air. As long as the wings have enough lift in the

U.S. Navy fliers called the Blue Angels perform amazing feats in the air.

upside-down position, the plane will stay in the air. First, however, the ailerons—the movable flaps near the tips of the wings—must turn the plane over. By moving the ailerons, the pilot can roll the plane over.

What is an automatic pilot?

An automatic pilot is a set of instruments that flies the plane without any help from the human pilot. The automatic pilot can keep the plane flying in the right direction. It can keep it at the correct height in the sky. The automatic pilot can be more precise than a human pilot.

If the weather is bad and rain, snow, or fog blocks the view, the pilot may use the automatic pilot. Pilots also use it if they are busy doing something else. Someday, flight may become completely automatic. Perhaps computers, not people, will guide airplanes throughout an entire flight.

131

Planes have become quite common. People no longer run out of their houses to look when a plane flies overhead, as they did in the early days of airplane flight. Even though seeing a plane is not an unusual event, planes are very important. Without them, life as we know it today would be very different. Here are some of the ways that planes at work help us.

PLANES AT WORK

AIRMAIL

When did people start using airplanes to deliver the mail?

Some early airplane pilots and balloonists carried mail as a stunt, but the first official United States airmail delivery was made in 1911. That flight was made by Paul Beck and Earle Ovington, who delivered mail from Garden City, New York, to Jamaica, New York, a distance of less than eight miles.

Earle Ovington was the pilot of the first U.S. airmail flight in 1911.

HOW NICE...
AN AIRMAIL
LETTER!

Today, almost all mail that travels more than 100 miles goes by air!

When did airmail really become part of the post office delivery system?

May 15, 1917, was the beginning of the first continuous airmail service in the world. Army pilots flew military mail from cities in Europe to New York City, Philadelphia, and Washington, D.C. Regular airmail service from the United States to Europe began in 1918. People paid much more to send a letter by air. Otherwise, the mail would go by boat, a much slower way of delivery.

BUSH PILOTS

What do bush pilots do?

Bush pilots fly to areas where very few people live. These areas are usually on mountains or in jungles or near the North and South poles. Bush pilots deliver food, medicine, and supplies. They take sick people to hospitals. There aren't as many bush pilots today as there used to be because there aren't as many isolated places.

Is bush piloting dangerous?

Often it is. Winds near the poles may gust up to 100 miles per hour. Isolated areas usually don't have weather stations, so a pilot has to judge the weather himself. Some places don't have airports or landing strips. A pilot might have to land in a field or even on ice. If the ice is too thin, the pilot is in serious danger.

A "crop duster" sprays chemicals over a field of crops.

PLANES FOR FARMERS AND FIRE FIGHTERS

How do planes help farmers?

Farmers need to spray their crops with chemicals to protect them from insect pests. The easiest way to do this is by plane. Farmers hire special planes that have big storage tanks to hold the chemicals. The plane flies low over the fields and sprays the chemicals on the crops.

How do planes fight fires?

Fire-fighting planes are like the planes farmers use to spray their crops. A fire-fighting plane has a storage area that can be unloaded over the fire. This storage area holds fire-fighting chemicals or water.

There is a Canadian plane that can suck up water from a lake! The water is then released over a fire.

PICTURES FROM THE SKY

How do photographers use planes?

There are many uses for aerial pictures—pictures taken from the air. Many travel brochures use aerial pictures. That is a good way to show all of a resort or even an entire country. The military takes aerial pictures of countries they believe are a threat. Such pictures locate the air and military bases of a possible enemy. Military technicians can study the pictures.

Pictures are good for mapmaking, too. An aerial photograph is almost a map all by itself. A mapmaker just copies what he or she sees and adds the right marks and names. Before planes were used in mapmaking, it was much more difficult to figure out exactly what a place looked like.

YOUR TURN TO FLY

> WAIT! DON'T LEAVE WITHOUT ME!

What is a scheduled airline?

Scheduled airlines fly planes every day at regular times. They are the ones who use the 400 biggest airports. There are about 13,000 airports in the United States. Almost 5,000 of these are public airports. Another 739 private airports are available for public use.

Are there any other airports?

Yes. There are private airports that can be used only by the members of the club or organization that owns the airport. The armed forces have more than 400 airports, which are open only to people in the military. Some military airports are used for transporting people and equipment, and others are used for trying out new planes.

One of the world's busiest airports is the Chicago O'Hare International Airport. In 1991, 110 planes took off every hour around the clock!

CHAPTER 16

SKY PATROL

Planes are extremely important to the armed forces. Some planes carry tanks and soldiers. Fighter planes attack other airplanes. Many new plane designs and ideas came about, unfortunately, because of war. Countries at war wanted the newest weapons to defend themselves.

IN THE BEGINNING

When were planes first used in a war?

Airplanes were first used for war in October 1911. During a war between Italy and Turkey, an Italian pilot flew over enemy lands to see what the people were doing there. Then the Italians decided they could use the planes to drop bombs. A few days later, another Italian pilot dropped four grenades over Turkey. He also scattered leaflets that urged the people to surrender.

WORLD WAR I PLANES

How were planes used in World War I?

In World War I, which took place from 1914 to 1918, some planes were used for observation. The Allied and the Central forces used the planes to spy on each other. The Allied forces were made up of Great Britain, France, Russia, Italy, and the United States. Germany, Austria-Hungary, Turkey, and Bulgaria made up the Central powers.

Each plane carried two people—a pilot and an observer. The observer made notes on enemy troops. Neither side wanted enemy planes to spy on them, so the observers started carrying rifles to shoot at other enemy planes.

This is a model of the Fokker Eindecker, which you can actually build from a kit!

What was the first true fighter plane?

A Dutchman named Anthony Fokker designed planes for the Germans. He solved an important military plane problem. The first machine guns put on planes would shoot holes in the planes' propellers. Fokker solved this problem by linking the gun and the plane's engine. Because of his idea, the gunfire missed the propeller every time. This plane was called the Fokker Eindecker, and it was the first true fighter plane.

The Spad was one of the fastest and strongest planes in World War I.

What were some of the other World War I planes?

A French plane called the Spad was the most popular. There were more Spads in World War I than any other plane. The Spad was very fast and strong. Another French plane was the Voisin. The Voisin was a plane that had a cannon mounted on the front and a gun mounted on the right-hand side of the cockpit.

What is a flying ace?

The term *flying ace* comes from World War I. An ace was any fighter pilot who shot down five or more enemy planes.

THE FAMOUS WWI FLYING ACE STRIKES AGAIN!

Here's a photo of the type of plane the Red Baron flew.

Who was the Red Baron?

The Red Baron of Germany was one of the greatest flying aces of all times. His real name was Baron Manfred von Richthofen (RIKHT-hoe-fun). He shot down 80 planes during World War I. The Allied ace who came closest was a Frenchman named Paul-René Fonck who shot down 75 planes. Richthofen was called the Red Baron because his plane was painted bright red. Baron von Richthofen was killed on April 21, 1918.

The Red Baron wasn't always a great pilot. On his first solo flight, he had to make a crash landing!

What are dogfights?

Dogfights are airplane battles in the sky. They were common during World War I, when squadrons of 10 to 20 planes fought each other in the sky. The planes twisted and turned in many directions as each pilot tried to shoot the enemy. A pilot would try to get behind an enemy plane before firing his guns. This kept him safe from bullets, but close enough to hit the enemy.

140

WORLD WAR II PLANES OF GERMANY, JAPAN, AND THE ALLIES

How were planes used in World War II?

More planes were made and used during World War II than at any other time. The war, fought from 1939 to 1945, was between the Allied and the Axis powers. The main Allied powers were the United States, Great Britain, and the then Soviet Union. Germany, Italy, and Japan were the Axis powers. Germany's plan was to have many planes fly over and bomb enemy countries. Then, the army would finish the fight. They called this the Blitzkrieg, meaning "lightning war."

The small British fighter, the Hurricane, helped Britain beat Germany in the Battle of Britain.

What were some of the World War II planes?

The Stuka was a small German dive bomber. It was the star of the Blitzkrieg. It dropped heavy bombs one at a time and hit more Allied ships than any other plane. German bomber planes were clobbered in the Battle of Britain by small British fighters called Hurricanes and Spitfires. These planes were very fast and could spin and turn easily.

141

What was the Japanese Zero like?

The Japanese Zero was a fighter plane that didn't have much power and wasn't very well protected. However, like the Hurricane, it could climb and turn

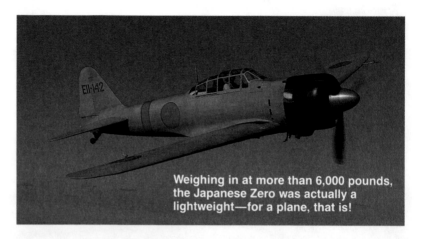

Weighing in at more than 6,000 pounds, the Japanese Zero was actually a lightweight—for a plane, that is!

very well. The heaviest model weighed only 6,025 pounds—about one-half the weight of U.S. Navy fighters. The Zero could reach speeds of 350 miles per hour. This was 20 miles per hour faster than any U.S. plane at the time. Some of the Japanese Zeros were flown by pilots called kamikazes.

Japanese kamikazes wanted to die for their country. When Japan started losing the war, kamikazes steered their planes into the decks of ships. The pilot would die, but the plane and its bomb damaged the enemy's ship.

I NEVER GO ON A MISSION WITHOUT MY BLANKET.

What planes were used against Japan?

One Allied plane that fought against the Zero was a Navy fighter called a Hellcat. With six machine guns and an engine that could deliver 2,000 horsepower, the Hellcat was a strong opponent for the Japanese Zero. Heavy armor plating gave the Hellcat protection against the Zero's two machine guns and two cannons.

Another Allied plane, the Boeing B-29 Superfortress, was the best bomber in World War II. The B-29 could carry 20,000 pounds of bombs and had ten remote-controlled machine guns. This was the type of plane that dropped nuclear bombs.

JET PLANES IN THE MODERN MILITARY

What is a jet plane?

A jet plane is an aircraft that has jet engines. When fuel is burned in a jet engine, it gives off hot gases. The gases shoot out of the back of the engine in a stream called a jet. The stream rushing out toward the rear makes the plane move in the forward motion we call thrust. Think of a toy balloon filled with air. If you suddenly let go of the stem, the balloon will zip away. Air rushes from the stem in one direction, pushing the balloon in the other direction—just like the jet plane.

How fast can a jet plane go?

One jet reached a speed of more than 2,193 miles per hour, but most jets can't go that fast. Most passenger jets travel at about 570 miles per hour.

What planes have been made since World War II?

Many planes have been built since World War II. In the Korean War, the North Koreans had Soviet MiGs, and the Allied forces had Sabres. These new jet fighters had sleek, modern designs. Jet bombers were made shortly after that. New planes were being invented more rapidly than ever. Soon, planes were going faster than the speed of sound. At sea level, the speed of sound is usually estimated to be 735 to 750 miles an hour. Because air density varies at different altitudes, the speed of sound varies.

HERE'S ANOTHER NEW MODEL, READY FOR FLIGHT!

Chuck Yeager stands next to Glamorous Glennis, the plane in which he broke the sound barrier.

Who was Chuck Yeager?

Charles "Chuck" Yeager, an Air Force pilot, was the first person to travel faster than the speed of sound. On October 14, 1947, he flew an X-1 rocket plane at 670 miles per hour, or Mach 1.015. The word *Mach* is a measurement of air speed. Mach 1 equals the speed of sound.

Because no one had ever broken the sound barrier, many people were afraid that dangerous things would happen to the pilot who attempted to do so. Some thought that any plane that tried to fly so fast would break apart. Others thought that the instrument controls wouldn't work. Yeager was willing to risk these dangers. His bravery paved the way for the supersonic flights of today.

Yeager's plane, the *Glamorous Glennis*, hangs in the National Air and Space Museum, by the Wright brothers' *Flyer I* and the *Apollo II* spacecraft.

What is the B-52 Stratofortress?

A giant jet bomber called the B-52 first flew in 1952. It was later used in the Vietnam War in the 1960s to drop as many as 100 bombs at a time. The B-52 flies at 400 miles per hour and is the oldest jet bomber still flying.

A pilot guides the super-fast F-16 into a turn.

What is the F-16?

As planes got bigger and bigger, they became more expensive as well. Working for the U.S. Government, one company designed a smaller jet, called the F-16 Falcon. This plane is so fast, it can reach Mach 2 and it has only one engine! The plane uses a computer to help the pilot fly the aircraft. Plans for future F-16s include using a voice-activated computer that will allow the pilot simply to tell the plane what to do.

What is the Stealth bomber?

The Stealth bomber is a U.S. military plane with a special advantage—it cannot be detected by radar. Its flat, smooth design, as well as materials that absorb radar, help to weaken radar signals. Instead, fuzzy or tiny signals are sent back to the enemy. Such weak signals are hard for the enemy to identify. The Stealth bomber can be used for secret spy missions or bombing raids because the enemy can't detect it.

STEALTH BOMBER

After taking off without a runway, the Harrier keeps climbing straight up into the sky.

What is the Harrier jet fighter?

The Harrier is a military jet with some special abilities. The Harrier can take off and land straight up and down without using a runway. This makes the Harrier valuable for fighting and transporting in areas that don't have runways or long flat spaces of land. The plane can hover, or stay in the air without moving, and can fly at almost the speed of sound. It can also carry more than 9,000 pounds of weapons!

146

What's that strange thing zooming overhead? Can you name that plane? From helicopters to a triangle-shaped plane, the sky is filled with all kinds of machines!

NAME THAT PLANE!

PROP PLANES

What is a prop plane?

The *prop* in *prop plane* is short for propeller. Prop planes have propeller engines rather than jet engines. A prop plane has blades in the front that spin around. These blades make up the propeller. The propeller helps to move the airplane forward.

CHOP
CHOP
CHOP
CHOP

How fast can a prop plane fly?

The speed of a prop plane depends on the size of the plane and how many engines it has. The single-engine six-passenger Piper Malibu Mirage, a popular prop plane for private use, has a top speed of 300 miles per hour. Pilot Lyle Shelton holds the prop plane record at 528 miles per hour.

HELICOPTERS

Are the blades on a helicopter called propellers?

No. Helicopters have rotor blades. These rotor blades are like wings that spin around on top of the helicopter. By spinning very fast, they pull the helicopter up in the same way that wings lift a plane. By tilting the blades, the pilot can move the helicopter forward or backward. If the pilot doesn't tilt the blades at all, the helicopter can stay in one place.

Because a helicopter can go straight up and down, it doesn't need a runway. A helicopter can even land on the roof of a building!

Who invented the helicopter?

About 500 years ago, a famous artist and inventor named Leonardo da Vinci (lay-un-AR-doe duh VIN-chee) drew pictures of a helicopter. He never built it. The first helicopter wasn't put together until this century. In 1939, Igor Sikorsky (EE-gore sih-CORE-skee) designed and built the first helicopter that worked.

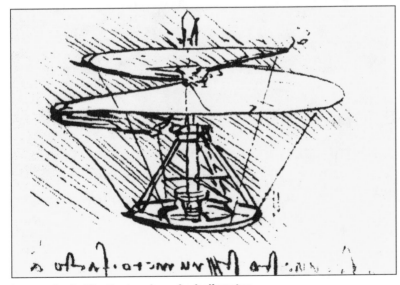

Leonardo da Vinci's drawing of a helicopter

What is a convertiplane?

Today, the military uses an aircraft called a convertiplane. A convertiplane is a plane that takes off and lands like a helicopter, but flies like a plane when it's in the air. This makes it easy for the plane to land and take off without a runway. Convertiplanes cost more to build than regular airplanes.

149

THE SST

What is a sonic boom?

A sonic boom is the noise made by a super-sonic airplane. *Super-sonic* means traveling through the air faster than the speed of sound—about 1,100 feet per second. When a plane is flying, waves of air build up in front of it. When a plane flies faster than the speed of sound, the waves become cone-shaped. The plane is inside the tip of the cone. A cone-shaped air wave is called a shock wave. When the cone sweeps over the ground, it makes a loud noise called a sonic boom. Over a period of time, such loud noises can damage ears.

A sonic boom can break windows and crack walls!

What is the SST?

SST stands for supersonic transport. SSTs fly faster than the speed of sound. Most planes don't fly nearly that fast. The Russian Tu-144 and the French and British Concordes are supersonic planes. The Concorde flies at about 1,019 miles an hour. A Boeing 747, which is not supersonic, flies at about 595 miles an hour.

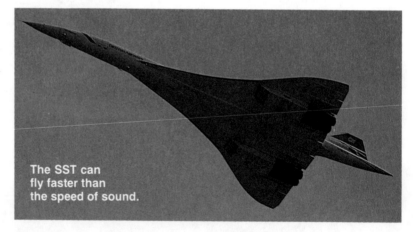

The SST can fly faster than the speed of sound.

What does the SST look like?

The SST is shaped like a dart. The wings are thin and swept back. When planes fly at supersonic speeds, air pressure against the fast-moving plane becomes very strong. The SST's nose comes to a sharp point so that the plane can cut through the hard pressure of the air. The body of the plane is only 9 feet 5 inches wide. This narrowness helps the plane cut through the air quickly. The SST has specially designed wings called deltas. These wings help the SST reach its supersonic speeds.

SEAPLANES AND AMPHIBIANS

Special floats on a seaplane enable it to land on water.

What is a seaplane?

A seaplane is an airplane that can land and take off on water. Under its body, a seaplane has long, tube-shaped floats instead of wheels.

Can a seaplane land on the ground?

No, but there are planes called amphibians (am-FIB-ee-uns) that can. An amphibian is a seaplane that has wheels that can be lowered for a ground landing. This plane was named after the animals known as amphibians. Frogs, toads, and salamanders are all amphibians. They live part of their lives in water and part on land.

WELL, I SEE YOU'RE READY TO LAND ON EITHER THE GROUND OR THE WATER!

GLIDERS

What is a glider?

A glider is an airplane without an engine. It is usually towed up into the air by an engine-powered airplane. The two are connected by a tow rope. When the rope is released, the glider flies through currents of rising air called "updrafts." The air pushes the glider up. When there is no wind, the glider lands.

Strapped into his harness, this hang glider pilot floats through the air.

What is hang gliding?

Hang gliding is a popular American sport. The person gliding wears a harness attached to a glider. The glider looks like a huge triangular kite. Its widest point is about twice as long as a car. There is a control bar so that the pilot can steer.

How does a hang glider work?

The pilot usually holds on to the glider and races down a hill into the wind. A more experienced pilot might jump off a cliff. The wind lifts the glider into the air. A hang glider can travel about the speed of a car on a busy street. A person learning to hang glide usually flies about as high as a house. After a while, an experienced pilot may take the glider up higher.

A parasailor gets help from the wind and a power boat.

Which sport combines sea and air power?

The sport of parasailing, made popular in Hawaii, combines aspects of hang gliding and water skiing into a fun air sport. The parasailor rides a parachute that is pulled by a motorboat and lifted into the air. The parasail is attached to the motorboat with a strong cable that is controlled by people in the boat. On some boats, the cable can be as long as 600 feet, giving you the same view you'd get from a 60-story building.

153

PLANES WITHOUT WINGS OR TAILS!

HEY, WHERE ARE THE WINGS?

How does a plane without wings fly?

The HL-10 is a wingless plane. It flies by rocket power. It travels at a speed of 610 miles per hour as it climbs into the air. When it reaches its flying height, the HL-10 moves forward at 1,200 miles per hour—faster than a supersonic plane.

What plane flies without a tail?

A plane called the Northrop Flying Wing, first built in the 1940s, had no tail. It didn't have a body, either. It was just two big wings put together. The pilot and crew sat in the cockpit located at the point where the two wings met. The tips of the wings were swept back. The plane was very thick in the middle. Some models reached speeds of 200 miles an hour!

It's not a big bird—it's the flying wing!

In 1959, French inventors flew a Coleopter, an amazing wingless craft that looked just like a flying saucer!

154

VULCAN AND VOYAGER

What other unusually shaped planes are there?

The Avro Vulcan, first flown in August, 1952, is a plane that looks a bit odd. It's a big triangle. The wings form two points of the triangle, and the nose forms the third point. In most planes, the tail assembly is behind the wings. In the Avro Vulcan, it lines up with the wings.

The Vulcan is 111 feet wide and 97 feet long. It was used as a bomber and had a crew of five.

THE VOYAGER

What is the Voyager plane?

The Voyager is a plane that was built by two pilots, Dick Rutan and Jeana Yeager, who believed it was possible to fly around the world without refueling. Specially designed to save fuel, the *Voyager* has a huge wingspan of 110 feet, flexible wings that can move 30 feet up and down, and 17 fuel tanks. These design features allowed the two pilots to circle the world in nine days, in December of 1986, without ever once touching down.

SUPER FLIERS OF THE FUTURE

What is the Hypersonic transport?

The Hypersonic transport is a plane being built by both the U.S. government and private aircraft makers. When completed, the Hypersonic is expected to reach speeds of up to Mach 25, 25 times the speed of sound. In comparison, the SST flies at *only* Mach 2.2. Other nations, including France and England, are working on similar superfast planes.

Hypersonic
Transport

Will everyone own planes in the future?

No one knows for sure what the future will bring, but there's a good chance that many people will use planes instead of cars. These planes will have to lift off like helicopters because there isn't enough room on Earth for everyone to have a private runway.

Have any planes for individual use been invented?

A scientist named Paul Moller has developed a plane called the Moller Merlin 200. It can rise straight up in the air and can go about 400 miles per hour. Its inventor claims that it can even take off from water.

The Merlin 200 can be filled up at an ordinary gas station!

DID YOU KNOW...?

Skydivers form a star pattern.

• Skydiving is a popular modern sport. Skydivers jump out of airplanes and do stunts in the sky. They do loops, turns, barrel rolls, and more. Sometimes a group of skydivers will hold hands and form a ring.

When skydivers get close to the ground, they open their parachutes to slow down their fall. Before skydivers open their parachutes, they can float through the air at 200 miles an hour! That's nearly four times as fast as a car on a highway!

• Many people have managed to swim across the English Channel, but Bryan Allen was the first person to pedal across in an airplane! He did it in a human-powered airplane called the *Gossamer Albatross*. It was made of plastic and piano wire. In June 1979, Bryan made the 23-mile channel trip.

On April 23, 1988, another pilot flew from Crete to mainland Greece in a pedal plane. The pilot was a Greek cycling champ named Kanellos Kanellopoulos. He covered 74 miles in his trip across the Aegean Sea.

• A big airplane may use more than 300,000 pounds of fuel on a long flight. That much fuel could fill a mid-sized swimming pool!

SNOOPY FOR PRESIDENT

● Some planes can write messages in the sky. These planes carry a tank that holds a mixture of chlorine gas and the chemical element titanium. This mixture makes smoke, which the pilot turns into puffy white letters in the sky.

● Every year at Wittman Airfield in Oshkosh, Wisconsin, pilots from all over the world attend the Experimental Aircraft Association Fly-In Convention. It is the world's largest flying event. Nearly 15,000 aircraft and one million people attend. Many of these airplanes have been built by their owners. For eight days, Wittman Airfield becomes the busiest airport in the world.

● Air Force One is the radio code for any plane that carries the President of the United States. There are two planes that have been specially made for the President and his staff.

● The Anglo-French Concorde is a small, narrow plane that doesn't look like it will go very fast or very far. But looks can be deceiving. This supersonic jet carries passengers across the Atlantic Ocean in half the time of regular jet planes. It's possible to eat breakfast at home in the United States and eat real French bread for lunch in Paris—all on the same day!

I KNOW IT'S NOT AS GOOD AS THE FOOD ON AIR FORCE ONE, BUT...

There's much more to discover in Snoopy's World.
If you've enjoyed *Earth, Water and Air*,
you'll want to read...

How Things Work

People and Customs of the World

Land and Space

Creatures, Large and Small